PULP

AND

OTHER PLAYS

Contemporary Theatre Studies

A series of books edited by Franc Chamberlain, Nene College, Northampton, UK

Please see the back of this book for the other titles in the Contemporary Theatre Studies series.

PULP
AND
OTHER PLAYS
BY
TASHA FAIRBANKS

Edited by

Gabriele Griffin
Leeds Metropolitan University, Leeds, UK

and

Elaine Aston
Loughborough University, Loughborough, UK

Routledge
Taylor & Francis Group

LONDON AND NEW YORK

First published 1996
by Harwood Academic Publishers.
Reprinted 2004
by Routledge,
2 Park Square, Milton Park, Abingdon, Oxon, OX14 4RN

Transferred to Digital Printing 2004

British Library Cataloguing in Publication Data

Fairbanks, Tasha
  Pulp and Other Plays. – (Contemporary
Theatre Studies, ISSN 1049–6513; Vol. 15)
  I. Title II. Griffin, Gabriele
  III. Aston, Elaine IV. Series
  822.914

ISBN 3–7186–5744–9 (hardcover)
ISBN 3–7186–5745–7 (softcover)

Front cover photo: *Curfew*. Jude Winter as Wonder Woman
Photo: Anita Corbin, with her kind permission

CONTENTS

INTRODUCTION TO THE SERIES

Contemporary Theatre Studies is a book series of special interest to everyone involved in theatre. It consists of monographs on influential figures, studies of movements and ideas in theatre, as well as primary material consisting of theatre-related documents, performing editions of plays in English, and English translations of plays from various vital theatre traditions worldwide.

Franc Chamberlain

LIST OF PLATES

INTRODUCTION

SIREN THEATRE COMPANY (1979–89)

Siren Theatre Company was founded in 1979. The women who created the company—Jane Boston, Tasha Fairbanks and Jude Winter—came together in Brighton, after an initial phase of campaigning for women's rights in mixed street theatre. As was the case with other alternative groups earlier in the 1970s, such as The Women's Theatre Group, the *agit prop* street theatre origins provided the impetus for a more permanent company formation.

Siren was founded as an all-women, lesbian collective committed to producing work concerned with women's and, more specfically, lesbian issues. As their company policy stated:

> The content of Siren's work relates very explicitly to the position of women in our society: how women occupy different social positions according to our class, disabilities, race, creed and sexuality, and how struggles can be waged from these various points against the institutions of oppression. Having said this, however, we utterly refuse to be hived into the ghettoized category of 'women's theatre'. It is too convenient a slot for those who wish to minimize our ideas and prevent our participation in 'mainstream' theatre. The point of departure for our work is, naturally, from our position as women, but the questions we raise and the concepts we challenge have universal impact. (Siren Policy Statement, 1986)

At the outset, Siren's shows were heavily influenced by the women's involvement with the punk movement and their music origins in the all-women rock bands Devil's Dykes and Bright Girls. The sharing of different performance skills (Jane Boston and Jude Winter had originally been more involved with music; Tasha Fairbanks with performance), and helping each other to develop new ones such as mime, dance and ventriloquism (see *Now Wash Your Hands, Please,* 1984/5), reflected the ethos of their collectively managed company, and their commitment to a performance aesthetic which challenged mainstream traditions of 'straight' acting. Their inaugural show, *Mama's Gone A-Hunting* (1980/1), for instance, was described in the programme notes as using 'drama, dance, mime, comedy (both verbal wit and visual slapstick), plus contemporary rock music, to explore some of the historical roots of women's lack of equal opportunity today'.

The company's work was significantly informed by radical feminist politics, as encoded in the ideas of writers such as Mary Daly for example, who looked to women withdrawing from heteropatriarchy to focus on a woman-centred structuring of ideas, energies, and relations (see, for instance, Daly's *Gyn/Ecology*, The Women's Press, 1979). This coincided with the moment when the white, middle-class, heterosexual agenda of the Women's Movement was being critiqued by the identity politics of groups of women whom it had failed to represent: by white working-class women, by black working- and middle-class women, by all lesbian women, by women of diverse ability, etc. (for further discussion, see *Feminist Review*, No. 31, Spring, 1989). What the company set out to do with their non-traditional performance skills, was to find ways of theatricalizing radical feminist ideas. This represented a challenge not only to the dominant political, social and cultural values, but also to the more mainstream views of the Women's Movement. In an interview with the editors, Jude Winter recalled the stir which the radical feminist perspective of *Mama's Gone A-Hunting* created: 'We were saying things that were threatening, certainly quite threatening to women in the Women's Movement such as suggesting that women should leave men and consider the possibilities that being with other women offer' (*Feminist Theatre Voices*, Loughborough Theatre Texts 1995).

Siren Theatre Company set itself up to challenge its audience and as contemporary reviews of their work make clear the audiences were indeed challenged. Thus a review of *Curfew*, one of the plays reproduced in this volume, stated 'Siren's new play is an angry and challenging sci-fi allegory about male violence against women' (*Spare Rib*, March 1982, p. 42). Similarly, when Siren toured *From the Divine* the reviewer, Liz Horsfield, stated 'when I went to see [this] show… I thought I was in for an undemanding couple of hours, where I could sit back and slip my mind into neutral. I wasn't prepared to work, but I got a shock. Not that it wasn't really entertaining, but to catch all the double meanings, connections and layers in it you really have to be on your toes' (*Spare Rib*, June 1984, pp. 42–3). It was the very complexity of Siren's work which lead another reviewer, Manny, to write of *Pulp*: 'what McCarthyite witch hunts and Thatcherite Britain have in common for lesbians is the stuff *Pulp* is made of. The story is not important, the play is significant' (*Spare Rib*, January 1986, p. 33). The same reviewer went on to celebrate *Pulp* with the statement: 'this is a feminist play *par excellence*, brilliantly acted, refreshing, hilariously entertaining'. Interestingly, this reviewer also complains about Siren relying 'so much on American material'; but it is perhaps this very fact which makes *Pulp* one of the plays particularly relevant to both a British and North American context.

INTRODUCTION

Siren's early shows such as *Mama's Gone A-Hunting* and their second production *Curfew* (1982/3) offered a critique of heteropatriarchy and male violence against women. Increasingly, however, the group focussed on woman/lesbian-centred energies. *Pulp* (1985/6), the second play in this anthology, demonstrates the company's move towards an exploration of lesbian roles and, most importantly, lesbian glamour and desire. Lesbian performance and the representation of desire has proved a significant challenge to the male gaze of the mainstream stage (discussed, for example, in Jill Dolan's *The Feminist Spectator as Critic*, University of Michigan Press, 1988). *Pulp*, which Jude Winter described as 'probably our greatest hit' (*Feminist Theatre Voices*), and which played for 82 performances, many of them sold out, is an indication of how important the treatment of lesbian fantasy and desire was/is to a spectating community of lesbian women.

Also in the mid-1980s Siren were concerned to take issue with Thatcher's Britain, to look 'into the external environment, into the politics around us, into maleness, masculinity, often opposed to it or discussing it' (*Feminist Theatre Voices*). This concern is represented in the third play in this volume, *Now Wash Your Hands, Please*.

Like many of the 'alternative', collective theatre companies in the 1970s, Siren began by having all group members contribute ideas on a topic for dramatization, but after their second production, *Curfew*, they moved towards a more skills-orientated method of working. This meant that the initial group discussion and pooling of ideas would be developed by company members taking on more clearly delineated roles. Whilst all the women were still performing at this stage, Tasha Fairbanks began to focus her attention more firmly on the writing, and Jane Boston and Jude Winter concentrated on the music. However, the initial inspiration for a project was always collectively arrived at, and this remained with the company throughout their collaborative rehearsal and performance processes.

As regards the plays in this volume, *Curfew* comes from the early phase of collaborative scripting, whereas *Pulp* and *Now Wash Your Hands, Please* are representative of the later phase when Tasha Fairbanks took on a more clearly defined role as writer.

The gradual move towards skills-orientation was also reflected in the style of the company's work. In the early shows the feminist message came first, and theatrical style was a secondary consideration. However, Siren were always concerned to make their shows visually stimulating and fun to watch. Simple sets, like the climbing frame in *Curfew* for example, encouraged them to make imaginative use of their bodies as performers: to find physical ways of playing. Sometimes style was dictated by genre: *Pulp* played with the generic expectations of the Raymond Chandler thriller, and *Hotel Destiny* (1987/8), a 'lesbian western', made use of the performance conventions of Country and Western.

As the company moved away from their early phase of message-orientated theatre, style became more important to them. When Hilary Ramsden became the fourth member of the company, she brought with her a style of anarchic comedy rooted in physical theatre training. (Hilary had trained at the Desmond Jones School of Mime.) Encountering her style of playing influenced the company in moving more towards a physical style of performance. This was most apparent in the company's final production, *Swamp* (1989), which was directed by Clare Brennan who had worked with the mixed physical theatre company Théâtre de Complicité. *Swamp* portrayed three Greek fates, who, as Jane Boston explained, have lost their purpose in life, and are 'looking to be active again, to take an active role in decision-making and the world at large' (*Feminist Theatre Voices*). The three fates worked through repeated patterns of physical gestures and movements, demonstrating their frustration at not being able to break the patterns and to initiate change. In particular, the company found a different way of working with the set, as working physically also required the performers to play with, and to create, the set as part of the workshopping and devising processes.

Sets in earlier productions, like, for example, the climbing frame in *Curfew*, as previously mentioned, had also generated imaginative theatrical play. The 'minimalist set of a single climbing frame, painted silver against a black backdrop', however, was not just an aesthetically significant 'staging fashion' in the early 1980s, but bespeaks the material conditions under which women's touring companies operated in the 1970s and 1980s, when Arts Council and other sources of funding were minimal, and women's theatre groups found state support hard to come by. Only two women's theatre companies, The Women's Theatre Group (now renamed The Sphinx) and Monstrous Regiment (now defunct) have been awarded regular Arts Council funding. For each of their projects, Siren received only small amounts of funding from South East Arts and from some regional arts associations, all guarantees against losses. In between productions the women had to take on other work in order to earn enough money to create another show. Lack of regular financial support makes it difficult to sustain a creative output, or indeed to keep a company afloat, as Jill Davis points out with regard to the underfunding of lesbian theatre workers in her introduction to *Lesbian Plays: Two* (Methuen, 1989). This makes Siren's ten-year commitment to lesbian theatre, during which time they produced nine shows, all the more remarkable.

Not until *Swamp* were the company ever in a position to pay themselves wages. Ironically, *Swamp* was the first and last show to receive project funding from the Arts Council. Funding for a gay Restoration piece, which Siren were planning to tackle subsequently as a joint venture with an all-male gay company in order to raise the profile of gay theatre work under threat from Clause 28, was not forthcoming. At this point, the company members of Siren began to think about separate career directions. Since then, Tasha Fairbanks has pursued her career as a playwright; Jane Boston teaches theatre; and Jude Winter and Hilary Ramsden have formed a new company, Dorothy Talk.

Not only is it the case that lesbian theatre has been poorly funded, but the number of lesbian plays published is also extremely low. In the introduction to Methuen's first anthology of lesbian theatre, Jill Davis notes that, in the volumes of 'sister' *Plays by Women*, only two of the plays tackle lesbian subjects (Methuen, 1987). It comes as no surprise, therefore, to find that Siren's plays have not, until this volume, appeared in print. This anthology of three plays represents a long overdue recognition of the company's work. Moreover, now that women's theatre is, finally, being taught and represented in educational contexts, it highlights the need to have more lesbian theatre texts made available in published form for study and performance.

The three plays chosen for this volume reflect the diversity of Siren's work. The selection is not presented chronologically. Rather, *Curfew* is twinned with *Pulp* to show the development from a radical feminist critique of heterosexuality and male violence, to a woman-centred emphasis on the creative energies of lesbian culture. The third play, *Now Wash Your Hands, Please*, which chronologically came before *Pulp*, shows Siren's different, but related, concern to create a political theatre in opposition to Thatcher's Britain.

CURFEW (1982)

Looking at *Curfew* more than a decade since its first production, the effect is of the strange made familiar, the familiar strange. The play has a framing opening and closing scene which *Startrek*-like, and from a 'technologically advanced civilization of matriarchs', projects the rest of the play 'into the future'. Utilizing terms gleaned from music such as 'treble' and 'octave' as names, these scenes with their focus on an 'energy recharging centre for women' are strongly reminiscent of the feminist sci-fi that was popular in the early 1980s, for example Sally M. Gearhart's *The Wanderground* (Women's Press, 1985), and found its expression in the Women's Press feminist sci-fi series. Here women created a utopian idea of a harmonious world of women, in tune with each other and the universe, against a backdrop of heteropatriarchal oppression which appeared swiftly to be moving towards the destruction not only of women but of the world at large. Indeed, one interesting and relevant companion read to this play might be Margaret Atwood's heterosexually inflected *The Handmaid's Tale*, first published, not long after *Curfew* surfaced, in 1985.

Curfew has an overtly political content which takes on two issues: women's relation to the state, and women's relation with each other. Both concerns have their immediate historical background in second wave feminism (as the phrase goes) in which women fighting for 'equality' found themselves successfully lobbying for changes in the laws which would entitle them to abortion under certain conditions, equal pay, equal opportunities, freedom from discrimination on sexual grounds, etc.

The future charted in *Curfew* is a bleak one in which a big-brother type of regime rules over the lives of all others, and women, especially lesbians, have been driven underground where they attempt both to continue with their lives and to resist or align themselves with the repressive state powers which seek to regulate them. Lesbian community, nostaligically evoked by one of the characters as an imaginary meeting of famous lesbians of *herstory* (Sappho, Pentissilia, Queen Christine, Alice B. Toklas and Gertrude Stein, Radclyffe Hall, Rita Mae Brown) in the lesbian club which is the setting for the play, has been all but destroyed. For the 40-year-old lesbian club owner Charlene this means trying to live in part in the past and, in part, attempting to arrange herself with prevailing conditions by paying off 'the Menace' to keep them off her and her lover Tracey's backs. Tracey, in the meantime, is involved with the women's underground movement which offers resistance to the regime through blowing up the central powerhouse and other forms of activism.

The atmosphere generated by the defunct club (which, it has to be noted, none the less remains a meeting place for the women) is reminiscent of the 1950s McCarthy era with its persecution of those suspected of 'anti-American' activities which included lesbians and gays. It compares very interestingly with the 1990s retro-reclaiming of 1950s nightlife and lesbian and gay bar scenes in recent plays such as Gay Sweatshop's *Stupid Cupid* (1993) and Neil Bartlett and Gloria's *Night after Night* (1993), in which—in contrast to *Curfew*—the atmosphere is nostalgic and optimistic. In *Curfew* the nightmarish and oppressive atmosphere of the club is suggestive of imminent violence and violation in ways evoked in descriptions of the '50s lesbian bar scenes in Joan Nestle's *The Persistent Desire: A Butch-Femme Reader* (Alyson Publications, 1992). This is heightened and reinforced at sound level by the sound of 'the Menace' banging batons against railings as they walk past the club. It is further invoked by the sense of persecution that all the women feel and express and, to some degree, inflict on each other.

The play presents the way in which living under heteropatriarchy is divisive in splitting different groups of women from each other so that the coalition-building energies they need to effect change are fragmented and diffused through mutual suspicion and inability to trust each other. The play focuses on three female characters: the lesbian couple Charlene and Tracey, and the heterosexual feminist Fi. Their interactions with each other rehearse the arguments women in feminism have had concerning their differential relations with, or separateness from, patriarchy. Fi, as a heterosexual feminist with an emotional investment in her relationship to a man, has to negotiate between her commitment to him (the primary and immediate source of her oppression) and her commitment to other women, particularly lesbian women who refuse any dependence on men, be it economic, emotional or sexual. The difficulty of this negotiation, which generates distrust from both sides and the necessity to deceive on her part, results in Fi's nightmarish breakdown in Scene 11 in which she finds herself confronted with patriarchy in the shape of a representative of one of its institutions, the church, who accuses her of being female and tempting. In this nightmarish scene, allusions to Cinderella, Chinese foot binding, sadomasochism, the (incestuous) abuse of young girls and the general sexual violation of women through rape and sexual assault are combined and condensed into a terrifying scene which moves rapidly from Fi attempting to find a comfortable shoe to her being cast as the object of a snuff movie, a pornographic film in which the woman, sadistically portrayed, is killed off in the act of sexual exploitation. This scene, projecting women's actual abuse by men within patriarchy surfaces, in rapid escalation, a large number of issues which throughout the 1980s and in the 1990s remain highly topical and offer an instance of the familiar made strange but being oh-so-familiar. Witness the issues of child sexual abuse, women's sexual exploitation by men (this issue was in the early 1980s dominated by the 'Yorkshire Ripper' case, and an interesting comparison read to this scene is Pat Barker's *Blow Your House Down*, Virago, 1984), debates about sadomasochism, etc.

The escalation of Fi's nightmarish breakdown scene is exploded by Tracey coming to Fi's rescue, similar to the way in which the figure of Wonderwoman seemingly comes to the rescue of Tracey in a previous scene in which Tracey is having a nightmare. This scene prefigures and parallels Fi's breakdown scene in that Tracey, too, finds herself persecuted and prosecuted by a member of institutionalised heteropatriarchy, someone from the legal system, who turns into a 'comic baddy' as the stage directions describe him. The prosecutor's language reflects the way in which the rape of woman, the violation of the land and colonialism derive from similar impulses of aggression, domination and devastation to maintain heteropatriarchal power. This comparative stance has formed one basis for feminist lesbian activism such as the women's camps at Greenham Common and ecofeminism.

Heterosexual Wonderwoman, played by the woman who also plays Fi, 'turns' on Tracey and, rather than rescuing her, makes to go off with the incredible hulk, a member of 'the Menace': but enter Calamity Jane, who confronts Wonderwoman in her fall from feminist-lesbian grace. Significantly this scene, which ends the sequence of Tracey's nightmare in Scene 9, does not end in a resolution of the conflict between Calamity Jane's lesbian separatist stance and Wonderwoman's heterosexual one; rather, both state their positions and neither wins the other over. By refusing simplistic solutions and, instead, raising questions about women under heteropatriarchy which the audience is invited to consider, the play adopts the style of Brechtian *Lehrstück*, a teaching play designed to activate the audience's critical faculties while entertaining them at the same time. In so doing, the play also makes use of a variety of alienation devices. The nightmare and the breakdown scenes function in a way which opens up the relationship between fantasy and reality, and the way in which reality comes to haunt the mind, resulting in nightmares and mental breakdown. These scenes also allow the augmentation of particular positions, their distortion and distention for effect and as effect. The use of Wonderwoman and Calamity Jane, for instance, both figures from other popular cultural traditions and well known to a wide range of audiences, transposes the question of women's relations with each other under heteropatriarchy into different and quasi-mythical dimensions: it re-states the issue outside a realistic time frame, thus both making it strange and enabling the seeing of it as familiar by asking the audience to relate Wonderwoman and Calamity Jane's exchanges not only to those between Tracey and Fi but also to ones between lesbian and heterosexual women outside the theatrical context. It reminds one of the famous and still much debated discussion of 'Compulsory Heterosexuality and Lesbian Existence' by Adrienne Rich which predated *Curfew* by two years.

As a theatre piece by a lesbian theatre group, *Curfew* maintains the women's theatre tradition of being entirely woman-centred. On-stage male characters such as the prosecutor and the priest in the nightmare and breakdown scenes are played by actresses. This has several interesting effects. For one thing, it reverses an old practice of men playing women, thus banishing the latter from inhabiting a public space. In *Curfew* women occupy all the visible space but that space is designated as 'underground', 'on the margins', with off-stage male voices intruding and disrupting that space. The play thus suggests that in a heteropatriarchal society, even when men are not physically present, their absence can still operate as an intrusive presence, haunting women's nightmares as well as dreams, and shaping women's lives. This inescapability is the source of the greatest anxiety which the play projects.

The use of these figures as well as Charlene's nostalgic reverie about a meeting of famous lesbians from different *her*storical moments, apart from acting as an alienation device, also reflects a feminist tradition of unearthing women who have been hidden from main/malestream history and establishing continuities across time and space in women's experiences of heteropatriarchy. This device has been used in other plays by women, especially feminist, playwrights; its most famous version is probably the first scene of Caryl Churchill's *Top Girls* which appeared in the same year as *Curfew* (1982). However, where *Top Girls* draws on high cultural referents such as Isabella Bird, a Victorian lady traveller, and Pope Joan, *Curfew* utilizes on stage only figures from popular cultural traditions. These figures function as carriers of generic traditions such as the comic strip and the western and thus highlight one of the ways in which lesbian cultural production, starting from socio-cultural margins, has sought to claim cultural space by appropriating mainstream popular genres and rewriting them for/within a lesbian cultural tradition. From lesbian appropriations of pulp fiction (see Ann Bannon's currently newly famous *Beebo Brinker* series from the 1950s, for instance, reprinted by the Naiad Press, Tallahassee), also dramatized for the stage in Bryony Lavery's *Her Aching Heart* (Methuen, 1991), to the rise of the lesbian detective novel/thriller in the 1980s and '90s, lesbian cultural production has established the re-writing of mainstream popular genres from a lesbian perspective as one of its subversive strategies for questioning heteropatriarchy and inserting itself within it. Although such a causal relation may be too easy to evoke, one might argue that this move has been very effective, as evidenced in the current 'gaying' (not uniformly celebrated) of mainstream culture—witness, for example, the notorious k.d. lang-Cindy Crawford spread in *Vanity Fair*, the 'lesbianized' fashion photography of mainstream fashion magazines, and the 'lesbian theme' in mainstream soap operas such as the British *Brookside*.

PULP (1985)

Pulp shares a number of stylistic and thematic concerns with *Curfew*. It has two plot lines, associated with different time zones and places. However, whereas in *Curfew* the framing device is offered as optional and can be either included or abandoned in any given production, in *Pulp* the two plot lines are interwoven through the time travel of one of its characters who inhabits both time zones. The fact that she is capable of functioning in both suggests—as did the references to Wonderwoman, Calamity Jane, and the famous lesbian figures in *Curfew*—the continuities which exist across time and space in lesbians' experiences of living of under heteropatriarchy. The two time zones used in *Pulp* are 1950s North America where, as was hinted at in *Curfew*, a McCarthyite atmosphere dominates, and Britain in 1985 which is constructed as not being dissimilar to the 1950s in the U.S.A. In both countries, in both times, lesbian women and gay men are regarded as potential threats to the state—as they are socially, culturally and economically marginalized due to their sexual preference; they are regarded as potential victims of blackmail and therefore a possible threat to the security of the country. Both *Curfew* and *Pulp* deal with the issue of how you live as a lesbian in a society which vilifies homosexuality. In *Curfew*, the answer, as the title suggests, is to go underground, living in a state of permanent besiegement and anxiety of discovery which leads to a sense of oppression permanently preying on the individual lesbian's mind.

In *Pulp* this problematic is further explored. Thus the 1950s-America plot line shows one lesbian character, Dolores, on the run from her family and husband; another lesbian character, Magda, deprived of her career as a film star because she is suspected of being a lesbian; and two further lesbians, a reporter and a private detective, living precarious lives in semi-self-employment, whereby they negotiate their needs to earn a living and survive with their wish to protect other lesbian women from being hunted down. Distrustful of one another, these lesbian women are forced to co-operate and reveal themselves to each other in the name of survival.

The 1985-Britain plot line offers a somewhat different position. Here two lesbian women, both employed by 'a British government security organization', co-habit in secret and on the basis that their relationship is not known. Under self-imposed curfew, their lives are disrupted when the younger of the two, Dagmar, supposedly begins to be resistant to the idea of living under constant curfew. Ella, the older woman, is too afraid of risking her livelihood and career to disclose her lesbianism and breaks off her relationship with Dagmar. Gradually it transpires that Dagmar has been employed by the security organization to 'flush out' Ella but that, in the course of doing her duty so to speak, she has fallen in love with Ella. Ella, however, finds this hard to accept.

Ella and Dagmar's story is complicated through the introduction of another character, Monika, a German expatriate, who turns out to have been a guard in a concentration camp in Nazi Germany. About to be interned herself in one of these camps, she put on a Nazi uniform to protect herself and thus saw out the Second World War as a guard rather than as the prisoner she was destined to be. Monika encourages Ella to re-think her strategy for survival of living a life camouflaged and under curfew.

Pulp's central concerns are with the persecution of lesbians under heteropatriarchy, with issues of public and private morality, and with the notion of betrayal. Like *Curfew*, it makes the point that the oppression of lesbians has not changed over time, that to be lesbian means to be an outsider, to be constantly in danger of losing your livelihood, to be at the mercy of persecution from others. In so far as the late 1980s saw anti-homosexual legislation in Britain, and in 1994 a vigorous debate was fought in the House of Commons concerning the lowering of the age of consent among homosexuals, these plays are not so much prophetic as documentary, detailing an on-going situation of oppression of lesbians and gays in this society. Both plays also highlight the ways in which this oppression affects the individuals concerned, the degree to which oppression can become internalized to such an extent that the victimized person not only introjects this oppression but lives in accordance with it, even to the extent of reproducing these oppressive structures in her own behaviour. Magda's treatment of Dolores is shown to equal Ella's treatment of Dagmar: both women are incapable of positive commitments to their lovers, isolated in their sense of their own vulnerability to external oppressors. Here we have the re-surfacing of the personal as political whereby the ways in which political positions and structures regulate private lives is demonstrated and staged. In the case of the 1985-Britain plot line we are reminded of the case of Anthony Blunt, a homosexual and former Keeper of the Queen's Paintings, who in 1979 was revealed as a one-time Soviet agent (see J. Weeks, *Sex, Politics and Society*, Longman, 1981, p. 241). Blunt became one more symbol for British obsessions with the blackmail-ability of homosexuals who inhabit and therefore threaten the very institutions which supposedly guarantee the 'freedom' of all other individuals. In *Curfew* this role is exposed as a farce by the fact that the very institutions set up to protect the country's citizens operate though an internal system of oppression which encourages a state of 'unfreedom' for some of the country's citizens.

This issue of heteropatriarchal systems of oppression and their relation to lesbians is framed within a setting which, as the title of *Pulp* suggests, draws on popular cultural conventions, in this instance popular romance, *film noir* and detective fiction. This appropriation and re-working of these mainstream conventions from a lesbian perspective is achieved in part through a typecasting familiar (to a lesbian audience) from lesbian pulp fiction. Here we have the glamorous older woman (ex-film star Magda, reduced to singing in a seedy nightbar after losing her 'marketability' as a Hollywood star due to having to appear in front of a committee for un-American activities), the persecuted run-to-ground younger 'butch-ish' adoring lover, the lesbian detective, bumbling but 'good at heart' and caught between survival and empathy with other lesbians, the hard-nosed lesbian reporter, wordly-wise, and knowing what she wants. Siren Theatre Company told us when we talked to them (*Feminist Theatre Voices*) that they constructed *Pulp*, and especially the figure of Magda the ex-film star, in order to get away from the image of the lesbian as unglamorous, unfeminine, dungaree-wearing, with short hair. In the light of developments in lesbian culture since the mid-1980s when this play was written, especially as regards the revaluing of butch-femme style relationships, the nostalgic reclaiming of the 1950s in lesbian and gay communities, the emergence of lipstick dykes, lesbian ballroom dancing, and 'queer' culture in its parodistic and pastiche revisions of heterosexual as well as lesbian and gay (life) styles of the past and present, *Pulp* was a timely intervention which has not lost its import. On the contrary: much of recent lesbian theorizing, whether one thinks of Peggy Phelan's *Unmarked: The Politics of Performance* (Routledge, 1993) or Judith Butler's *Gender Trouble* (Routledge, 1990) and *Bodies That Matter* (Routledge, 1993), has, in a sense, picked up on points already made in 1981 by writers such as Monique Wittig in 'One is not Born a Woman' (*The Straight Mind and Other Essays*, Harvester Wheatsheaf, 1992) or even earlier (1929) by Joan Riviere, namely that womanliness as a patriarchal construct is a masquerade enacted by women to protect themselves from men in a system where the distribution of power is unequal and works to their disadvantage. *Pulp* suggests that lesbians come in many different guises and disguises, that the latter are forced on them by heteropatriarchy, and that this can lead to internal/ized oppressions among lesbians, and among women in general.

Differences among lesbians are presented in *Pulp* through its various characters. Magda, the ex-film star, is constructed as narcissistic, career-oriented and self-centred. Glamorous, desirable and desired by all the other women who swarm around her like moths to the flame, she embodies the larger-than-life screen figure akin to Greta Garbo and Marlene Dietrich, adored by lesbian and gay audiences, and (suspected of being) lesbian herself, about whom Jackie Stacey has recently written in *Star Gazing: Hollywood Cinema and Female Spectatorship* (Routledge, 1994). She appears to have a certain courage and ruthlessness, desired by but lacking in the characters around her, to pursue her own ends, and to come up trumps no matter what. The dream woman whom she presents to all those around her, women and men alike, is also a figure incapable of commitment, a dream precisely because she cannot be the 'reality' to others which the fantasy of her makes them wish for. This in itself constitutes, of course, a stereotype, and part of the pleasure of this play lies in recognizing such playing on stereotypes. It also underwrites the idea of a gap between fantasy and reality which is the basis on which one of the characters, Dolores, suggests—as the play then attempts to show by operating in two time zones—that one can live in two times zones simultaneously.

This idea replicates the notion that as a marginalized figure you inhabit two spaces at once, one which is hidden and one which is visible. However, in contrast to the assertion within the play that the hidden space is the fantasy and the visible space is the reality, as regards lesbian identity the play reverses this notion: the 'true' lesbian self, what one might term the reality, is hidden whereas a sexually non-identified or presumed-to-be heterosexual self (the 'false' self or fantasy) is visible—at least from the point of view of a heterosexist society. This has immediate implications both for the lesbian characters in the play and for an audience of the play: both are constructed as clue-seekers, as reporters or detectives who have to decode the signs they find in order to know what is fantasy and what is reality, what is 'true' and what 'false'. Heddy, the reporter's, and Kay, the private eye's roles in the play are thus replicated by the audience who are also encouraged to try to unravel the mysteries of a plot. As a strategy, this device relies on audience participation and recognition: the audience needs to be familiar with generic conventions and lesbian cultural traditions in order to decode the parodistic elements of *Pulp*, and there is pleasure to be had from the uncovering of the plot. The audience is thus offered particular subject positions by *Pulp* through the figures of the reporter and the private eye.

Both plots within the play, the 1950s and the 1985 one, show the disintegration of one lesbian relationship and the opening up of the possibility of another. In the earlier plot, the detective and the reporter end up with a new understanding of their similarity and mutual desirability; in the later plot, Ella is offered the option of teaming up with Monika. Both sets of characters are constructed as having gone through a learning process which, among other things, has encouraged the stripping away of disguises. What makes the two potential relationships possible is the fact that the people involved are not disguising themselves in relation to each other, that the pretence or fantasy that they have kept up or reserved for others, does not operate between them. The play thus makes a plea for the need of honesty as a basis for one's own integrity and for the possibility of sustaining a relationship. To be fully known (as Monika is by Ella when she reveals to her that she was a guard in a concentration camp) and to be loved none the less, is of course one of the great romantic fantasies but it is also, so the play suggests, the only basis for political action and change.

NOW WASH YOUR HANDS, PLEASE (1984/5)

The issue of political action and change is one which is central to *Now Wash Your Hands, Please*. The play uses the bizarre setting of a British Rail 125 Express train, which is secretly carrying nuclear waste, to take a satirical and hard-hitting look at class-divided Britain under Thatcher's government. The train functions as a metaphor for Tory Britain in 1984.

Looking at the play in 1994, a decade later, the critique of 1980s Conservative politics—the government's handling of the miners' strike, the privatization of public industry and national institutions, the 'us and them' divide-and-rule policies, the taxation measures which favour the rich and disadvantage the poor, and, indeed, the emphasis on the ideal pretend nuclear family—are depressingly familiar and highly topical. The current privatisation of British Rail, pit closures, punitive taxation measures, 'back to basics' family values, etc., mean that *Now Wash Your Hands, Please* could easily be revived in the 1990s with renewed satirical vigour.

The play's main thematic concern is with our perception of the world, and how 'seeing' things differently can help us to bring about political and social change. This thematic is voiced by the character Phyllis, a nuclear physicist, in her description of quantum physics:

> Just think—that enormous leap forwards from Newton's theory of the world as static and compartmentalized to the quantum theory—energy in constant motion, effecting universal change. Isn't it quite thrilling? But people are still clinging to outworn ideas when we're living in a quantum age, with all its endless possibilities. It's a crisis of perception.

Publicity information for the production of *Now Wash Your Hands, Please* elaborated on this point as follows:

Much of that 'crisis of perception' can be seen today in our modern political and social activity and the inflexible and outmoded institutions and concepts from which they emerge. Like the Newtonian physicists, are we approaching problems that demand a dynamic, interrelating world-view from a rigid, limited perspective?

Many people are saying 'yes'. But then how to bring about the revolution in perception that would enable us to make the quantum leap in our attitudes towards the world's 'insoluble' problems? How to communicate the ideas that would bring about such a profound shift in perception? This is the central theme of *Now Wash Your Hands, Please*.

The 'crisis of perception', the need to make connections and 'see' the world differently, is theatrically encoded and enacted in *Now Wash Your Hands, Please* on a number of different levels and through a variety of techniques. Like the quantum physicist, the spectator has to 'see' things differently. (Peggy Phelan develops a complex discussion of this point, in the context of Tom Stoppard's 'spycatcher-quantum mechanics-thriller' *Hapgood*, in *Unmarked*.)

In terms of feminism specifically, *Now Wash Your Hands, Please* addresses the issue of difference which arose as a consequence of 1980s identity politics. The feminist focus on identity, whilst necessary to an analysis of oppression, suffered from a tendency to highlight difference at the expense of unity. Rather than looking to the main (male) oppressors, this meant that the feminist agenda in the mid-1980s was primarily concerned with organizing around oppression specific to one particular group of women, but not necessarily uniting them on issues of common concern. *Now Wash Your Hands, Please* acknowledges difference, but also looks beyond it, and sees class as a vehicle for making connections between women (for further discussion, see Sheila Rowbotham *et al.*, *Beyond The Fragments*, Merlin Press, 1979).

To stop the Tory train, for example, the play demonstrates the need to find a common dialogue between oppositional characters here presented as Polly, a young working-class revolutionary, Phyllis, the middle-class nuclear physicist, and Bert/Bertha, a working-class railway worker. The overthrow of 'P.R.', 'Thatcher's right-hand man', depends upon being able to unite left-wing opposition in the struggle against the Tory oppressor. This is realized in the play which concludes with the surreal, utopian fantasy of flushing the Tory government down the toilet.

For the spectator to start making connections, and to 'see' things differently, *Now Wash Your Hands, Please* establishes a mode of theatrical representation in which nothing is what it seems. As everyone pretends to be someone else, identities shift and are destabilized. It becomes difficult to 'see' whom to trust; to know, with certainty, who is telling the truth, etc. The visual play of the 'real' and the 'disguised' are compounded by the verbal comedy of language. Through the figure of P.R., the control and manipulation of language, the arbitrarily imposed system through which we perceive and communicate in the world, is satirically exposed as a powerful weapon for transforming political lies into dangerous realities. For example, lies, deceptions, and perceptions are playfully treated in the 'appearance' of Bert/Bertha's mum's ghost. The comic and irreverent feminist parody of Shakespeare's ghost sequence in *Hamlet* is used to make visible Tory propaganda. The device of the ghost, a comic representation of the acknowledged 'unreal', is used to challenge the lies of the 'real'.

Disguise and identity also link to the issue of sexuality. Lesbian identity is repressed by dominant heterosexual and familial values espoused by Tory ideology. However, *Now Wash Your Hands, Please* celebrates and makes lesbian identity visible through the layers of disguise and comic play, and, at the same time, exposes the Tory myth of the 'nuclear' family. The alienation of what is perceived to be the 'ideal' sexual/familial 'norm' is achieved through using a number of critical distancing devices. In a blonde wig and high-heeled shoes, Polly uses the masquerade of femininity to hide her lesbian-feminist, revolutionary identity. Bertha, who cannot get a job as a woman, alienates gender construction by cross-dressing in a uniform of masculinity as the railway worker Bert. The myth of the 'Happy Family' is deconstructed by using dummies and the art of ventriloquism. Using manipulated dummies is an entertaining, but politically instructive way of critiquing the bourgeois concept of the family. In addition to the ideological work of this device, it opens up a whole range of comic play: for example, the Persil-packet-dummy 'mum' generates a number of jokes around government whitewashes and dirty linen washed in public, all of which have gained new currency in our 1990s 'back to basics' real-life political farce!

Where theatre is traditionally supposed to offer us an illusion of 'reality', the anarchic comedy of *Now Wash Your Hands, Please* uses the concept of illusion to expose the 'real' as one huge political fiction 'staged' by the Tory government. The politician's rhetoric (as performed by P.R.), and the biased 'right-wing-reality-making' powers of the media and press, are all subjected to scathing comic scrutiny. Satire, and the use of techniques such as ventriloquism, disguise, direct address, songs and electric rock music, etc., help to generate a performance energy which encourages the audience to critically 'see' through the lies.

In the 1990s we are still 'hurtling' (?) along on the Tory 125 express. Passenger inertia seems to have replaced any energy for change, and areas of common interest and activism are even harder to identify. If we are ever to stop the train, or ever to 'wash our hands' of the Tory government, then those connections which help us to 'see' the world differently urgently need to be made.

Gabriele Griffin and Elaine Aston

CURFEW

Devised by
SIREN THEATRE COMPANY

and

scripted by
TASHA FAIRBANKS

SONG LYRICS: JANE BOSTON AND COMPANY
COMPOSITION: JANE BOSTON AND JUDE WINTER

FIRST PERFORMED AT THE NIGHTINGALE, BRIGHTON, 1982

THE COMPANY

FI AND WONDERWOMAN: JUDE WINTER
TRACEY AND HUNK: TASHA FAIRBANKS
CHARLENE AND CALAMITY: JANE BOSTON
DESIGNER AND TECHNICIAN: DEBRA TRETHEWEY

THE PLAY WAS DIRECTED BY THE COMPANY

PERFORMANCE NOTES
The play has been performed in two versions:
1) With the first and last scenes, so that all the intervening scenes are a projection into the future by the highly technologically-advanced civilisation of matriarchs.
2) Without the matriarchal scenes. The play then stands alone as a violent, Expressionist sci-fi story of a woman's underground resistance movement in a repressive patriarchal state.

THE SETTING
Charlene's lesbian club, a once-noisy, colourful meeting place for women, but now a cold, cheerless basement, in a terrain of semi-derelict streets, barricades and barbed wire. There was no attempt made to create a naturalistic setting. We used a minimalist set of a single climbing frame with a swing, painted silver, against a black backdrop.

THE SONGS
The Wonderwoman/Calamity song and the Server/Priest song were both performed vaudeville style, as intrinsic parts of the action. The rock songs were performed by the actors, as a disruption of the narrative, and served as an alienation device to make political comment.

THE MAIN CHARACTERS
CHARLENE—Forties. She had kept the club for many years and her life once revolved around a nocturnal lesbian social life. She now earns her living by singing in a Patrolmen's bar. She abhors all revolutionary sexual politics and blames it for the present state of repression.

TRACEY—Mid-twenties. Charlene's lover, she is an active member of the resistance.

FI—Late twenties. A "manned" woman, she has joined the resistance, nonetheless.

A Karate Kata is a series of set defensive and attacking moves, performed against 3 or 4 unseen opponents.

CURFEW

SCENE ONE

THE MATRIARCHAL COMPUTER CENTRE

(A woman stands in the room, beside a large Cabinet. Smiling and breathing deeply).

COMPUTER: Goodday sister. This is your friendly computer. You are about to enter REWOP. REWOP is the energy recharging centre for women. REWOP absorbs energy from women all over the planet. This energy is then available to sisters present and future. You are about to become part of the energy flow. To receive energy you may step in now. Mind the doors, please. Pulse check, breathing rate. Stand by. We hope you are comfortable. Have a nice transference now.

(The lights around rewop flash on and off and there is a pleasant surge of synthesised sound that turns to an unpleasant jangle as it comes to a stop) We hope you had a nice transference. Please mind the step as you leave.
(She steps out of The Cabinet, flustered)

TREBLE: I didn't. Everything started to go sharp and out of time. I must communicate this presto. Octave, is that you?
OCTAVE: Treble, Hello. Is everything harmonious sister?
TREBLE: Octave, while in REWOP, I discovered... Discord *(They sing jarring chord)*
COMP: As computer in charge of REWOP...
TREBLE: In charge! There's no one in charge here. All responsibility is shared.
OCTAVE: Shared, therefore, diminished. Where did you learn that phrase 'in charge'?
COMP: From the bass ones.
TREBLE: From the men. Haven't heard of them for ages. Thought they'd all gone off somewhere.
COMP: They're back. 'In charge' is one of their new phrases.
OCTAVE: I've heard they've been lowering the tone completely. Their attitude to sharing for instance. They're saying... 'mine'.
TREBLE: Absolutely dotted!
COMP: Mine, mine, mine.
TREBLE: De-programme yourself of that word immediately.
OCTAVE: And seeing who's got the biggest stick.

3

TREBLE: Good galaxy, does it matter?

OCTAVE: And they have started to show sexual interest in us rather than in each other.

TREBLE: How off-key! What is going on?

COMP: We could find out. If you care to programme me for a computation, I could come up with a theory in precisely five seconds. Theory computation in A flat. (*Computer noises*)

TREBLE: Well!

COMP: The men are reversing everything!

TREBLE:
OCTAVE: REVERSING EVERYTHING!

TREBLE: Octave, please do not talk at the same time. I cannot stand choral works.

COMP: Would you like to know how I arrived at that answer?

TREBLE: No. Pianoissimo please, while we think. This could be serious, Octave. This could bring about total lack of harmony on a major scale.

OCTAVE: Where will it all end?

COMP: I can answer that question for you. There is an underused, and no doubt, rusty circuit on my microchip. The projection circuit.

TREBLE: We can look into the future, Octave.

COMP: Not strictly correct. We could project a future that might happen, if you programme me with all the givens. Stand-by for a projection into the future. We hope you are comfortable. Have a nice trip now.

(The lights of the computer room fade and the stage becomes dark with stark points of light for the song "Curfew")

CURFEW

The warning bell sounds
The curfew hour
All the boys go out to play
All the women must hide away

There's a chink of light
Where a woman's watching
One last look, and the curtain drops

She is out of sight, out of mind
A woman at home
Behind a drawn blind

CHORUS
Hurry hurry must get home (2)

CURFEW

Heart beat accentuate, pulse rate accelerate
CURFEW—and she is silent.

A woman is seated
Quietly thinking, the searchlight scans
Scans her very soul

Pinpoint probe
In a beam of light
The walls are breathing
They are listening

Her future's on file
Her dreams are on tape
Trapped on microfilm
She cannot escape
CHORUS

SCENE TWO

CHARLENE'S CLUB

(Charlene wanders around her club in a nostalgic reverie)

CHARLENE: Charlene's club, not what it used to be. All these years gathering dust. How many years since they shut us down? A club ain't no club without people. But I tell you something—I'm going to have a secret celebration which *they* will know nothing about. Because we'll keep it very quiet won't we girls?

(Suddenly she turns to welcome her ghostly guests)

Sappho, darling, always the first to arrive. And the last to leave. Pentissilia, darling your spear's so sharp, leave it at the door, but come right in. Christine, how nice of you to come, and all the way from Sweden, a string of broken hearts behind you. And Alice B, it's not often we see you here without Gertrude. What a lovely rose is a rose is a... Radclyffe, how severe you look tonight—Now that you're here this ain't no well of loneliness. Can I introduce you to... Rita Mae? Good, good. Do come in darlings, all of you, *(Suddenly afraid)* that is if no one is watching you and no one knows you're here. Walls have ears. Those sweet nothings can be a real giveaway to the wrong ear on the right wall. *(Conquering her fear)* Well what are you waiting for girls? The champagne is flowing, the orchestra is tuning up. *(Afraid again)* But keep it low. This is just the beginning, the first one. Let's not make it the last. We know what they will do to us if they catch us. But don't let me spoil the party. Chez Charlene's, Charlene's club, it's a little wonky but it swings...

(There is a knock at the door upstairs. Charlene puts off the light quickly and shrinks into the shadows)

TRACEY: *(Voice calling from above)* Charlene. Where are you?

CHARLENE: In the club.

TRACEY: *(Entering)* No one followed us. Put the lights on. What are you doing down here?

CHARLENE: *(Putting on lights)* I've decided it must be lived in again. *(She sees Fi)* Who is your companion?

TRACEY: Her sister name is Fi. She's a new member. *(Takes Charlene to one side)* She's manned...

CHARLENE: A manned woman in here! You must be crazy.

TRACEY: She's OK.

CHARLENE: *(Not convinced)* Really?

FI: *(Coming forward)* You must be Charlene. Tracey did tell me you'd be here. How interesting this place is. Trace said it was almost derelict...

TRACEY: *(Hurriedly)* She's reliable, no question.

CHARLENE: *(To Fi)* I am, of course, delighted to see you.

FI: Yes, delighted, of course.

CHARLENE: But I wasn't expecting company tonight.

TRACEY: I just wanted to tell you what was going on. The liberation group met last night. We've planned an enormous 'towning'...

CHARLENE: 'Towning'! *(She turns angrily away from Tracey)* What think you of the decor, Fi? A trifle on the baroque side, perhaps?

FI: *(Nervously)* Very baroque. But very nice.

CHARLENE: I've kept it exactly as it was when it was first opened. Except for the dust. Always the dust. *(She goes into a reverie)*

TRACEY: Charlene, listen to me please, I have news...

CHARLENE: Which I don't wish to hear. I shall turn a deaf ear.

TRACEY: You're impossible when you're in this mood. It's important. You have to know.

CHARLENE: I know only what I remember. And only what I remember is important to me.

FI: *(Animated)* It's funny the sort of things you remember. You know, I remember that before all this we were able to... *(Her eyes glaze over)*

TRACEY: Her memory flickers.

FI: *(As normal)* O but, how silly of me...

CHARLENE: And fades.

FI: I won't be able to go out tomorrow because I forgot to ask Jed to sign my day pass.

CHARLENE: I remember a time when there were no such things as day passes.

FI: Do you? O tell me. So few women dare to talk about it nowadays.

CHARLENE: And we didn't have to pretend to be manned.

TRACEY: Yeah, because everyone automatically assumed that we were manned. Things are just clearer now, that's all.

CHARLENE: No, we could walk freely all over the sector. Even at night.

FI: You were allowed to go out alone at night?

TRACEY: No one actually stopped us, no. But we crept like shadows, afraid of the footsteps behind us. Didn't we, Charlene?

CHARLENE: (Off hand) Did we? I don't remember.

FI: At least you didn't have to pretend to be a man to go out alone at night. Every time I go through the Control Point wearing men's clothes, I think "will it work this time"? But it always does. The Menace must be really stupid.

TRACEY: No, they've just got one version of what a woman looks like. If you don't match up to it then you're a man.

CHARLENE: Oh, you always exaggerate, Tracey. It was a tolerable life. It has existed. In my mind it still does. Fi, you could walk in here out of the night and there'd be a room full of women.

FI: (Taken aback) Of women? O!

CHARLENE: The special heat of women's bodies, you know?

FI: O yes, eh, yes.

CHARLENE: Feet moving rhythmically to the music. The thrill of that ancient ritual of woman singing woman. O Tracey, I can't wait to have my little celebration. To have this place filled with women again. All that smoke, all that desire; all those thoughts, all that fire.

FI: All there at night together? All those women, together? All that smoke, all that fire, all that noise! They'll have you trapped in here together.

TRACEY: Charlene thinks it will be OK. She has certain 'friends'.

CHARLENE: Hardly friends!

TRACEY: Acquaintances then who can help. But you've got to be careful, Charlene.

CHARLENE: O money speaks louder than brotherhood, Tracey. Fortunately, Fi, one can buy co-operation. A blind eye for the night.

FI: You negotiate with the Menace?

TRACEY: We deal with a few, to survive.

CHARLENE: Don't we all? You, I should imagine, more than us.

FI: No never.

CHARLENE: I don't believe you.

FI: I don't. Jed is neutral. So are all his friends.

CHARLENE: Ah, yes, the neutral man.

FI: I never even have to speak to the Menace. Unless they speak to me on the street, of course. But then I always try not...

(An unpleasant menacing noise is heard from outside. They all turn towards IT)

FI: What was that?

CHARLENE: My friendly local patrolman. He's late. Probably drunk as usual.

TRACEY: He passes every hour from now on.

FI: Every hour! That's very often.

CHARLENE: The Central Powerhouse is across the street. The Menace jealously guard it.

TRACEY: *(Getting up)* We'd better go. Goodbye Charlene

(Tracey goes to kiss Charlene tenderly but Charlene draws impatiently away)

FI: *(Sotto voce)* O. I never realised you were weirdo, twisted, queer, maladjusted, neurotic, man-hating, inadequate, lonely, lesser beings. *(The lights fade)*

TWO WOMEN SONG

Two women walking hand in hand
Who are they? (2)
Two women walking without men
Who are they? (2)
Two women—where are their men?
Why are they? (2)

There's a tremor underground
The earth is in danger of shaking—
quaking
The seas are boiling
The sands are shifting
Underneath the rocks are breaking—
making
An unnatural disaster.

Two women walking hand in hand
Who are they? (2)
Two women walking without men
Who are they? (2)
Two women—where are their men?
Why are they? (2)

How does it make you feel?

Angry
Scared

Nervous
Turned on
Turned off
Aggressive
Threatened
Indifferent
Never

Are you glad you're not?
Do you ever think you might be?
Do you sometimes wish?

SCENE THREE

(Stark lighting as Tracey performs part of a Karate Kata signifying female strength and power. The kata turns into a direct action, Tracey creeping from shadow to shadow suddenly freezes. Fi enters cautiously, picks up something from the ground and throws it with all her strength. The lights go out).

SCENE FOUR

CHARLENE'S CLUB

(The lights go up on Tracey and Fi as Charlene enters in a rage)

CHARLENE: Madness. Attacking the Central Powerhouse!
TRACEY: You've seen it?
CHARLENE: I didn't need to see it. They're talking about nothing else at work.
TRACEY: Good.
CHARLENE: Good? So close to home?
TRACEY: Every Powerhouse is being hit.
CHARLENE: You know my danger.
TRACEY: We can't make exceptions.
CHARLENE: Do you care?
TRACEY: O Charlene.
CHARLENE: My existence depends on connections I have made with the Menace. But these are fragile, they could snap at any time.
FI: We were very careful.
TRACEY: It won't be associated with you.
CHARLENE: They are all on the alert. What does that mean for my celebration?

FI: You could postpone it. Even cancel it... We don't really need...

CHARLENE: What! She has no idea what it is to be starved of women's company.

TRACEY: She's right. It's too dangerous to have a celebration now. Charlene, there'll be plenty of time for celebration after we've won.

CHARLENE: After we've won! Now where have I heard those words before? Eh?

FI: Have you attacked them before?

TRACEY: Of course we've attacked them before. Did you expect us to have done nothing all these years?

CHARLENE: You and your friends unleashed the Menace all those years ago. Things were bearable until then.

TRACEY: They wouldn't have stayed that way for long.

CHARLENE: They might have.

TRACEY: Every day some little freedom was removed. Nothing much to make a fuss about you'd say, but added together...

CHARLENE: But why violence?

TRACEY: You tell the Menace that.

CHARLENE: There are other ways.

TRACEY: What other ways? They have always controlled the other ways. Our ideas were being diluted, absorbed, Managed. We reacted in the only way we could.

CHARLENE: And then the Managers became the Menace, and we have barely survived since.

FI: *(In a small voice)* I never knew you'd attacked them before.

CHARLENE: Are you prepared this time?

TRACEY: We've never been so strong...

CHARLENE: Or are yor the same rabble you always were?

FI: Why didn't I know about this?

TRACEY: *(Impatiently)* Do you expect the Menace to publicise our attacks?

CHARLENE: *(To Fi)* You wouldn't have. It's all hush-hush, brushed under the carpet. No publicity. Only some women disappear quietly in the night.

FI: To interrogation centres?

CHARLENE: Who knows? Some to return, though never quite the same again, while others... and life gets a little closer to the edge for all of us. *(Fi shivers miserably)*

CHARLENE: O you're shivering. Let's not get downhearted. What shall we talk about to cheer us all up? O, I know, my party. To which no guest will come, because there will be no one left to come. *(She pauses dramatically and looks at them)* Just a room full of ghosts, with myself as host, moving through the shadows. Filling the empty cup. Your health, ladies. Let's celebrate. *(Bitterly)* Let's raise the dead. The last waltz. Take your partners for the Danse Macabre. And slowly the shadows moved in time. *(She leads a terrified Fi around the room in a slow waltz)* Your hands are so cold, my dear. They're like ice.

FI: *(Pulling away and crying)* But you can have parties at any time. They're not that bad with neutral men. You hardly even notice them. You can talk on your own. You can even dance on your own.

TRACEY: *(Thoroughly out of patience)* Stop it, both of you.

CHARLENE: *(Pleading)* Tracey, I'm afraid. Stop now, before you go too far.

TRACEY: The Menace have already gone too far.

CHARLENE: You've got to wait.

TRACEY: Too late to wait.

(The lights fade on the scene, spotlight on Charlene, singing)

YOU'VE GOT TO WAIT

SUNG BY CHARLENE

You've got to wait
Or they will decimate you
When you pounce
You'll need every ounce
Of strength
That you
Can get

So play it slow
Till you're ready to go
Don't let it show
You're planning to overthrow them

Hide your intent
Don't get so pent-up
Throw them *off* the scent
'Cos they're no gentlemen.

Don't give yourselves away
You've gotta live today
I won't be so scared
If you take care
Prepare yourselves

You're off the track
You'll never crack them
If you attack
The odds are stacked against you
Don't be rash
Don't move
Till you can smash them

11

SCENE FIVE

JED AND FI'S HOUSE

(Fi is standing on a stool cleaning the window to the garden. As Tracey enters unheard, Fi is waving cheerfully to an unseen Jed)

TRACEY: Hello, Fi.

FI: *(Letting out a little scream)* Tracey!

TRACEY: The door was open...

FI: What are you doing here? You're not staying. You can't stay. Jed's here.

TRACEY: Where?

FI: Out in the garden.

TRACEY: That's alright then. *(Looking about her)* So this is the happy home.

FI: I told you never to come here. It's too dangerous. *(Her attention is claimed by a voice from the garden)* *(Calling out the window)* It's alright dear, it's only a friend of mine. No one important.

TRACEY: Thanks a lot.

FI: I didn't mean... *(Calling)* Yes, OK. I'm sure she'd love one. *(To Tracey)* He says would you like a rose, he'll cut you one to take home. *(Tracey is about to use an expletive)*

FI: *(Hurriedly)* Yes, she'd love one dear.

TRACEY: Fi, will you get down from there a moment and come and talk to me.

FI: *(As Tracey moves towards her)* No! Come away from that window. I don't want him to see you.

TRACEY: I don't particularly want to see him.

FI: He might... he'll think you look a bit weird.

TRACEY: Weird? What do you mean weird?

FI: *(Hurriedly)* I don't mean weird. It's just that you don't look like..., well you don't act like... O for goodness sake, Tracey, he can tell a mile off that you're not manned. He'd know right away.

TRACEY: So?

FI: Well, I'm sure he'd like you if he got to know you.

TRACEY: I don't give a...

FI: He just wouldn't give himself the chance.

TRACEY: I thought this Ned was supposed to be neutral.

FI: Jed, actually. He is, he's really sympathetic. *(Her attention is claimed again from outside)* *(Calling)* No, Jed, she won't be able to stay that long. We'll just chat. Yes, I'm sure she'd love to another time. *(To Tracey)* He said would you like to see his video cassette of early women's theatre?

TRACEY: What the hell's he doing with it?

FI: It's a collectors' item, apparently.

TRACEY: What a set up. Where does Mr Neutral think you go off to at night? Yoga classes?

FI: No. Discussion groups.

TRACEY: And he doesn't know about you and the 'townings'?

FI: (*Shocked*) Of course not. That's the work of extremists... he thinks.

TRACEY: Yes, well, it's best that he goes on thinking that.

FI: Yes, yes, it's best. Look Tracey, please go. He might come in from the garden at any moment.

TRACEY: Not till I've told you what I came to tell you. Sit down, Fi. If you'd been to Charlene's...

FI: (*Abruptly*) I couldn't. I've been so busy. For one thing, Jed's been off work. He's had a bad neck.

TRACEY: What a shame.

FI: I couldn't just go out and leave him...

TRACEY: Why not? What's more important?

FI: It's not a question of that.

TRACEY: Yes it is.

FI: (*Indignant*) You ask too much from people, Tracey. I'm not as single-minded as you. I've got a life to lead as well. I can't just drop everything. It's different for you, you haven't got a home and someone to love. I've got responsibilities... (*Calling outside again*) The begonias? O, I don't mind where you put them.

TRACEY: (*Sotto voce*) I'll tell him where...

FI: (*Calling quickly*) O that's a lovely idea, Jed. (*Turning to Tracey*) Look, Tracey, you know about the new bill?

TRACEY: The Protection of Female Persons from Disorderly Gatherings.

FI: Well, it means we can't meet as usual, so there's no point in me going to Charlene's.

TRACEY: I know we can't meet as usual. That's what I came to tell you. The meeting today is at the Mothers' Centre.

FI: The Mothers' Centre. O no.

TRACEY: Give your name at reception. Tell them you're there for the Ante-natal class. It's in Room B.

FI: I can't. I can't go tonight. Jed's not well. (*Calling out of the window*) What's that, Jedsy. O dear, I never knew you could rub a hole in it. O, O I see. You're teasing me. I never can get jokes. Yes, yes, you're right. I mustn't put myself down. Sorry. (*Fi gets down from the chair dejectedly*)

TRACEY: You've got to go. You're giving the briefing.

FI: What!

TRACEY: You know the latest details. I've got to go and give the briefing to Unit K. Their representative disappeared the day before yesterday.

FI: To an interrogation centre?

TRACEY: They found her this morning. She's got a bad neck too. It's broken.

FI: *(To Jed)* O shut up! No, no, I didn't say that. Jed, I didn't mean... *(To Tracey)* Tracey, he's coming in. You must go.

TRACEY: Alright. I'm going. But everything depends on you, Fi. You've got to be there. *(She exits)*

FI: *(Calling after her)* You know I can't go. *(Lights fade)*

SCENE SIX

THE MOTHERS' CENTRE

(Fi is standing alone in a single light. She begins speaking nervously)

FI: Tracey couldn't be here today, so I'm going to give you the report back from the planning group. You can't hear me at the back?

(She mounts a platform and looks about her nervously. Gradually her voice gains confidence. She speaks, however, in a secretive, urgent voice as though to a private gathering)

FI: There've been some changes in the plans for attacking the powerhouse...

(Suddenly a beam of light sweeps the stage followed by the unpleasant noise of the menace and footsteps going slowly past)

FI: *(In a completely different tone of voice)* We're all concerned about the welfare of baby, but despite teething problems we're still going ahead. *(The noise of the menace passes by)*

FI: *(Leaning forward urgently)* We've thought of firebombing the Powerhouse. Yes I know we don't know what's inside it. It could be something highly explosive. We have checked the area. There's no one living nearby who could get hurt. *(The menace returns)* So mothers, we're talking about a bottle revolution. Breast is no longer best. Fill the bottle up with juice, 4 star if you can get it, 3 star at a push-chair. Plug the top with plenty of cotton wool and there we have baby's little cocktail. This should d-light easily and go down with a bang. And as for wind.... *(The sounds of the menace passes by)* Make sure it's in the right direction. The attacks must take place at the same time all over the sector. We don't want anyone to be early otherwise they'll be alerted and the streets will be full of rape groups. *(The sound of the menace returns)* So mothers, it's your baby now. Once more into the breech. *(The menace passes by)* *(Fervently)* And we'll soon have them crawling. *(Lights fade)*

SCENE SEVEN

(Tracey is seen in a single stark spot performing another part of the Karate Kata, defending and counterattacking against a number of imaginary opponents.)

SCENE EIGHT

CHARLENE'S CLUB

(Charlene is moving round the room, turning lights down. Tracey is taking off her boots)

TRACEY: What's the matter? The bulb gone?

CHARLENE: *(Soothingly)* Tracey, you're very charming tonight.

TRACEY: I can't stand dingey lighting. I can't see a thing now.

CHARLENE: Then touch, feel, try your other senses. How about some music, Tracey? Something low and slow. *(She goes over to the piano and tinkers with it caressingly)* No, it's not quite right. Don't you agree?

TRACEY: It's alright. Just keep it low, that's all.

CHARLENE: *(Picking up a guitar)* How about something with a Spanish flavour? Something to fire the blood.

TRACEY: What's all this in aid of?

CHARLENE: What a delicate turn of phrase you have. What this is in aid of is pleasure. Sheer unadulterated pleasure. A dirty word these days. *(Tracey grunts)*

CHARLENE: Are you tired?

TRACEY: Yes, I am actually. *(She yawns)* Fi hasn't called has she?

CHARLENE: *(With a dramatic chord on the guitar)* No, senorita, she has not.

TRACEY: *(Hopefully)* She might have called while you were out?

CHARLENE: She might. Can I assume you will be in for the rest of the night?

TRACEY: Yes. There's nothing else planned for tonight.

CHARLENE: *(Stops playing the guitar)* I'm so glad. I do worry about you, you know.

TRACEY: Don't worry. I was born under a lucky star.

CHARLENE: *(More seriously)* I do worry about you. Sometimes when I'm sitting here waiting, I wonder what I'd do if you never came back one night.

TRACEY: *(With an attempt at levity)* Well, I'm back tonight, ain't I?

CHARLENE: *(Recovering her poise)* O, the whole night. *(She returns to the guitar, romantically)* Cara mia.

TRACEY: Huh?

CHARLENE: (*Mimicking*) Huh? (*Tracey laughs*) Do I see a gleam of light on the horizon? Yes? No? Alleluya! I've got a smile out of her at last.

(*Tracey is visibly relaxing and an atmosphere of intimacy develops. Suddenly there is a loud rapping on the door upstairs*)

TRACEY: What's that?

CHARLENE: Must be the patrol. It's a bit early for this week's 'pay off'. (*Flippantly but nervous*) I shall have to complain. (*She exits upstairs*)

CHARLENE: (*Voice off*) Hello. (*Surprised*) O, I was expecting George. Is he sick?

PATROL: (*Voice off*) No, patrolman 365 accepted an early retirement. I'm the new patrolman from now on.

CHARLENE: (*Voice off*) O, I don't remember seeing your face before. I know most of them from this unit. I work in the patrol bar. I'm a singer.

PATROL: (*Voice off*) I know your details.

CHARLENE: (*Voice off*) Well thank-you for coming to introduce yourself. I'm sure we'll get along very well.

PATROL: (*Voice off*) That depends. There's been a lot of unrest lately.

CHARLENE: (*Voice off*) I have heard. It's disgraceful.

PATROL: (*Voice off*) Just opposite.

CHARLENE: (*Voice off*) I keep a look out. But of course working at night as I do. I hope you find them.

PATROL: (*Voice off*) We will. This is a big operation. We'll rip the sector apart. Remember we can enter here at any time. We'll find them and anyone who's aiding and abetting them, and ram home a lesson they'll never forget. Goodnight.

CHARLENE: (*Re-entering the club*) Accepted early retirement? What the hell is that a euphemism for? More to the point what did he tell them before he went? They know something. Or they suspect. That's obvious. (*Suddenly she sees Tracey sitting rigid*) Tracey? Tracey, what's wrong? It's alright, I've got rid of him.

TRACEY: (*Bitterly*) So I heard. I hate it. I hate to hear you being nice to those... It's disgusting. (*A silence*)

CHARLENE: I see. And I disgust you too, do I? But if I didn't do it my dear, I wouldn't be here now. And neither would you. My niceness allows you to be politically pure.

TRACEY: I'm sorry. I've got no right to say that.

CHARLENE: No.

TRACEY: Especially as it's me who's putting you at risk. I'm sorry. I think you're marvellous. (*She moves restlessly about the room*) They've obviously started making connections between the Powerhouse attacks and this club.

CHARLENE: (*Dryly*) Doesn't take a mind of genius. I knew it would happen sometime.

TRACEY: I shouldn't stay here then. I can't put you in any more danger.

CHARLENE: Don't be silly. Where would you go?

TRACEY: O, there's plenty of places.

CHARLENE: Fi's?

TRACEY: No, not Fi's. I don't think Jed would like that.

CHARLENE: Where then?

TRACEY: There's plenty of places.

CHARLENE: Theresa and Jan's?

TRACEY: Yes, that's a good idea. They always said I could go there if I needed to.

CHARLENE: (Impatiently) O don't play heroics. It doesn't suit you. At this moment you need someone you can trust completely. Who else have you got but me? You say Fi, she's your co-worker, but how can you be sure you can trust her? (Tracey moves away) What's the matter, Tracey?

TRACEY: I think Fi's... Well I'm not sure...

CHARLENE: Has she let you down?

TRACEY: Yes, I think so. She was meant to go to the Mothers' Centre meeting today but I don't think she went.

CHARLENE: Was it important?

TRACEY: Crucial.

CHARLENE: So this is what has been worrying you. Why don't you tell me about these things?

TRACEY: Because you never want to hear about the Powerhouse attacks.

CHARLENE: (Bitterly) I've never trusted manned women.

TRACEY: There are others in the organisation. They've always been alright.

CHARLENE: But it's not the same for them. It's not a matter of life and death. You can't go Tracey, I should just worry about you. And besides, there's nowhere else for you to go. (She puts her arm around Tracey tenderly. They begin to embrace)

SCENE NINE

TRACEY'S DREAM

(Tracey is falling asleep. As she does so the words of the patrolman echo in her ears accompanied by the noise of the menace)

PATROL VOICE: This is a big operation. We'll rip this sector apart. Remember we can enter at any time. Any time. We'll ram home a lesson they'll never forget. Goodnight. Goodnight. Goodnight.

(She falls asleep and dreams. In her dream a voice is hissing at her from the side. She wakes up with a start and sees she is on a stage, there is fairground music *playing and from the wings of the stage a comedian dressed as a colonel is beckoning to her and hissing)*

COMEDIAN: Get up you idiot, we're on.

(She begins to get up and as in a dream make her way to the wings)

COMEDIAN: Come on, hurry up.

(In the wings, to the fairground music, he puts on her a big red clowny dress and then pushes her on to the stage. He comes in after her, she pulls up short and he bumps into her)

COMEDIAN: *(To her)* You stupid bloody git. *(To the audience)* Good afternoon, gentlemen. At ease. Just a few words before we make the assault. We are fighting for the peace of mankind. We come to liberate not to devastate. We come to colonise not to civilise. Right, so much for the P.R., I need a volunteer to hold the map. *(He looks at Tracey. She has been mimicking him and generally playing the clown, or the clown's foil)* Come here, stop mucking about and hold the map. Gentlemen, *(He mimes giving her a map, she mimes unrolling it)* Gentlemen, you see before you a map of country X, study it, memorise it, digest it, think it, dream it. Because this is your battlefield and that's how you are going to win her. *(She has obviously unwound it so that it is in folds on the floor. He sees, raps her on the knuckles with his stick and she quickly rolls it up to the correct length)* We're calling this Operation Thrust. *(Pointing to the map which becomes parts of her body)* Up here—centres of population, depopulate. Down here—large areas of virgin forest, defoliate. In the middle—lakes, reservoirs, drinking water, radiate. Centres of production *(He points to below her stomach)* leave intact. We'll need them. Now, tactics—forcible entry, short sharp missions, quickly in and quickly out, plenty of rocket fire, fragmentation bombs. Makes one hell of a mess, but then we don't have to pick up the pieces. *(She has dropped the mimed map, and is trying to make her way silently off stage during the next bit)* Languages—don't worry about it, they can speak ours. *(He catches sight of her)* Besides they're a cheerful little people, and you can usually get a smile out of them. *(He catches her, squeezes her cheek and twists it. She smiles)* Remember, they're sly, underhand, and cunning. So beware. And if they think they can get away with it, they've got another think coming. We'll ram home a lesson they'll never forget.

(Suddenly the two stand quite still. The comedian has lost his brashness and has become a counsel for the prosecution. The two begin to perform a minuet with quiet dignity)

TRACEY: Hey, what about me?

PROSECUTOR: What about you? What are you doing? What have you done?

TRACEY: Done? Nothing. I've done nothing.

PROSECUTOR: You have valuable minerals, precious metals, on display.

TRACEY: Not on display.

PROSECUTOR: Do you bother to hide them? Cover up their existence?

TRACEY: No.

PROSECUTOR: So you flaunt them.

TRACEY: They're there. That's all. In the ground.

PROSECUTOR: Close to the surface?

TRACEY: Sometimes.

PROSECUTOR: Sparkling, glinting, glittering, tempting? Are you not deliberately provoking this sort of thing?

TRACEY: No.

PROSECUTOR: You've let investors in, foreign investors, mining for your ore, digging for your diamonds, sinking shafts for your… ?

TRACEY: Yes.

PROSECUTOR: So, you're not averse to them helping themselves.

TRACEY: Yes.

PROSECUTOR: Yes?

TRACEY: No.

PROSECUTOR: No? Did you say yes or did you say no? Do you mean yes or do you mean no?

TRACEY: It's different. I gave them permission. There were returns. This was an invasion.

PROSECUTOR: The alleged invasion. Did you know these men?

TRACEY: Some of them had come before—as ambassadors, advisers, businessmen, educators, scientists, …friends.

PROSECUTOR: You let them in? Opened doors to them? Accepted favours? Granted favours no doubt in return. And now you expect me to believe they turned into nasty, brutal aggressors? You say the countryside is torn apart… you have a large population, what sort of a struggle did they put up?

TRACEY: O a great struggle. But we were afraid. They threatened us with nuclear weapons.

PROSECUTOR: Did they show you these weapons? Did you actually see their nuclear weapons?

TRACEY: No. They're in secret, underground, moveable launching pads—somewhere.

PROSECUTOR: I see. Now I can't quite picture how it happened, this invasion. Would you care to reenact it for us?

TRACEY: No. I can't go through that again.

PROSECUTOR: Is that because it never happened? Was it real? Or are you imagining it? (*As his voice echoes that question she minuets around him and ends up with her arm about his throat*)

TRACEY: Is this real, or are you imagining it? (*He falls to the ground and crawls away*) Help. Help. (*Fi twirls in as Wonderwoman*) Fi!

WONDERWOMAN: No, not Fi, Wonderwoman!

TRACEY: Wonderwoman!?

WONDERWOMAN: What's the problem, sister?

TRACEY: I'm stuck in a nightmare and I can't get out.

WONDERWOMAN: Give me the facts. How did it all start?

TRACEY: (*As she moves offstage in a dream*) Well, I suppose it all started when this new patrolman came round to Charlene's club and threatened to force his way in. We heard this loud noise, you see and... (*Her voice tails off as she moves off stage*)

WONDERWOMAN: When I heard the clang of steel on steel, I knew it could only mean one thing—steel toe caps scaling iron drain pipes. My female intuition told me it must be the Menace trying to crack open a safe house. I sensed evil. (*A comic Baddy enters and mimes what she says in her running commentary*) Just as I thought—they are removing the tiles from the roof in order to uncover the loft insulation and penetrate the central heating system, into which they will then inject paralysing toxic nerve gas. A juvenile tactic. Aha, they've spotted me. Whoever you are you don't know me very well. If I can stop bullets with my bracelets, I certainly won't be done in by a few roof tiles. Goddess Diana give me your strength. (*She stuns him with an Acrobatic Kick. There follows a Comic Chase around the stage*) (*She steps back into the shadows, he looks for her*) They're stepping up their attack. Doesn't bother me none. I'll wait here and pick them off one by one. (*The Baddy pauses stage left, looks, takes off his hat, scratches his head, puts his hat back on and goes to the other side of the stage and looks. He takes off his hat. Wonderwoman comes behind, scratches his head. He puts his hat back on*)

BADDY: Thanks. (*Suddenly a look of surprise crosses his face. He swings round and sees Wonderwoman. They both jump back*)

WONDERWOMAN: Hunky Dory. My old arch enemy.

BADDY: Yep. You're looking at the master mind, the brains behind the brawn.

WONDERWOMAN: So we match our wits again. To the death this time Hunk.

BADDY: I'm gonna wipe the floor wid you. On your knees, Wonderwoman. (*He makes a rush at her and crabs her foot. Casually she flicks him away two or three yards*)

WONDERWOMAN: Don't speak too soon, Hunk.

BADDY: Prepare to meet your doom, Amazon. (*He rushes her again, she grabs his outstretched arm and twists it around behind his back pushing him away again*)

WONDERWOMAN: Brave words, Hunk. But you're not doing too well. *(Hunk looks in vain for his other arm)*

BADDY: Has anyone seen my hand? *(He eventually finds it, with an exaggerated start. Turning to Wonderwoman, he prepares to rush again, roaring like an animal)*

WONDERWOMAN: What a charming way with words. *(He rushes her. She gets him in a death grip. She holds his life in her hands but she can't do it. She lets him go)* This time Hunk, you're lucky.

BADDY: *(Taking her hand and slobbering over it)* No, this time sister, it's you who's lucky. *(He kisses it)*

WONDERWOMAN: *(Looking dreamily into his eyes)* O Hunk. You're incredible. *(They exit arm in arm)*

TRACEY: Hey, Wonderwoman, you're a disappointment. You've got a rotten script writer. You were supposed to be saving me from my nightmare, not go off with the Menace. You've just made it worse. I'll have to find another strong woman to help me. Let's see if I can remember my ABC of strong women. A, Anon. No, I think she's dead. B, Boedicea. No, she couldn't get her chariot down the alleyway. I know, Calamity Jane. *(Sound of harmonica and a voice off starts singing)*

VOICE OFF: O the Deadwood Stage is a coming on down the hill...

TRACEY: Calamity, where are you?

VOICE OFF: *(Singing)* Home, home on the range...

TRACEY: Well, could you come here to Sector 5. We need your help. One of the Menace has just stolen part of women's history.

VOICE OFF: *(Stops singing)* Which part?

TRACEY: Wonderwoman.

VOICE OFF: Never heard of her.

TRACEY: You know what it's about, it's the cooption of strong women.

VOICE OFF: Huh?

TRACEY: Look, they'll do the same to you. They'll say all the tough cowgirls in the West wore hooped skirts and baked apple pies for the men. *(Calamity Jane enters, six-shooter at her belt).*

CALAMITY JANE: Hey haw, let me at them yeller bellied rattlers. *(She gives a furious tuneful strum on her guitar and blows her harmonica)*

CALAMITY JANE: *(To audience)* Anybody here seen who stole Wonderwoman? Because iffen I catch 'em I'll whoop they're hides. *(She takes off guitar and harmonica, puts them down)* Got to get rid of these things. Girl's got to have room to move if a girl's got to do what a girl's got to do. *(She paces stage, looking into the audience twirling her six-shooter and scratching her behind)* Hell, something bit me. Something's wrong here, really wrong. Yep, something smells stronger than a skunk's fart. If I find out who stole Wonderwoman I'm going to beat the shit out of them. Ain't no-one better think they can make a fool out of Calamity. Why, I can kill a man at 500 paces and eat, drink, shit, play poker, bury my dead Gran'ma—God rest her soul—and all at the same time, Hee haw. I bet you I know who it was took Wonderwoman, that Wild Bill Hickup. I never did trust a man further than I could gob down a rattler's arse hole. Why, do you know what Wild Bill done to me? That Critter said he wanted to be my pardner and then he tried to... he tried to... (*She spits violently*) So I pumped him full of lead. Wouldn't you? Ain't that what a gal's right arm's for? (*Wonderwoman enters*)

WONDERWOMAN: (*Entering*) Calamity, how could you do that to a poor man?

CALAMITY JANE: You heard what he done to me. Anyway's who are you?

WONDERWOMAN Wonderwoman.

CALAMITY JANE: Jumpin' Jehosophats. Why, Wonderwoman, I thought you'd been rustled. Glad you managed to escape. Say, why don't you's and I's get together and get a posse up. We can whoop their hides together.

WONDERWOMAN: Calamity, you don't understand. I wanted to go with him.

CALAMITY JANE: You mean you wanted to... to... to... (*She spits violently*)

WONDERWOMAN: O Calamity, will you never learn? (*They begin a song and dance*)

SONG
WONDERWOMAN : A girl needs a guy it's as natural as apple pie
CALAMITY JANE : Why don't you tumble?
                        It will crumble and I'll tell you why.
                        The cream will turn sour
WONDERWOMAN : We'll have custard instead
CALAMITY JANE : There'll be bugs in the flour
WONDERWOMAN : But not in the bed
CALAMITY JANE : You'll be pastry without filling
WONDERWOMAN : Wonderwoman's willing
CALAMITY JANE : He's making a killing

CHORUS
WONDERWOMAN : He's here to stay (x3)
CALAMITY JANE : Quick get away (x3)

WONDERWOMAN : I'm all in a funk about Hunk, my knees turn to jelly
CALAMITY JANE : Hunk is a skunk, what he needs is a bullet in his belly
WONDERWOMAN : We'll ride into the sunset
CALAMITY JANE : You'll git yourself saddled
WONDERWOMAN : My life will be perfect
CALAMITY JANE : He's a snake—you'll get rattled
WONDERWOMAN : Losing him I couldn't bear
CALAMITY JANE : It's a grizzly life you'll share
WONDERWOMAN : O you're being so unfair

WONDERWOMAN : He's here to stay (x3)
CALAMITY JANE : Quick get away (x3)
WONDERWOMAN : I'll have Hunk's little babies and they'll all grow up
         like Hunk
CALAMITY JANE : I'd rather give birth to a prairie dog or be a monk
WONDERWOMAN : They'll be muscley and tanned
CALAMITY JANE : More Hunks I can't stand
WONDERWOMAN : They'll be heroes of our land
CALAMITY JANE : They'll be a Menace I'll be damned
WONDERWOMAN : Can you imagine what a life?
CALAMITY JANE : You wanna borrow my knife?
WONDERWOMAN : I'll be the perfect wife

CHORUS
WONDERWOMAN : He's here to stay (x3)
CALAMITY JANE : Quick get away (x3)

(Tracey runs on to the stage panic-stricken)

TRACEY: Calamity don't leave me. I'm still stuck in this nightmare. Hey, before you go, have you got any words of wisdom for a girl?
CALAMITY JANE: *(Voice far off)* Yep, when in doubt, pump 'em full of lead.

(Tracey goes back to the place where she originally fell asleep and takes up the same pose)

SCENE TEN

CHARLENE'S CLUB

(Tracey is asleep. There is a sudden knock at the door, Charlene goes to open it. You hear the voices off)

CHARLENE: Hello, Fi.
FI: Hello, Charlene. Is Tracey here?
CHARLENE: She's asleep at the moment.
FI: I won't be very long. *(Fi enters and goes to the sleeping Tracey)* Trace, wake up. Trace. Trace. You're like a hunk of stone.
TRACEY: *(Waking up)* Huh? What have you come back for? Didn't he like your apple pie? *(She peers through bleary sleep-filled eyes at Fi)*
FI: What?
TRACEY: *(Coming to)* You've got a nerve coming here.

FI: Yes, it was very risky, actually. The streets are swarming with guards. The patrols are checking all the day passes. It's almost as bad today as it was yesterday for the Mothers' Centre meeting.

CHARLENE: Why should that worry you? You were safe and sound.

FI: Well, yes, I've got a legitimate pass, but they were picking up women at random for questioning. Jed said even he would have thought twice about going out. So he thought it would be very dangerous for me.

CHARLENE: If it was dangerous for you, it was twice as dangerous for Tracey.

TRACEY: I managed it without too many problems.

FI: Yes, well, perhaps it was easier in this area. And anyway you've had more experience at avoiding the patrols.

TRACEY: There's only one way of getting experience.

FI: Yes. But for me it was very frightening. And anyway Jed...

TRACEY: Suddenly had a bad turn with his neck just as you were leaving.

FI: How did you know?

CHARLENE: Elementary, my dear.

TRACEY: And so you had to mop his fevered brow?

FI: Yes, I did. He's ill.

TRACEY: O Charlene, Jed's ill. We must send him a bunch of roses. Or would he prefer bloody begonias?

FI: Look, why are you being so nasty? What are you getting at me for?

TRACEY: Why am I getting at you?

CHARLENE: Fi, the whole plan might have failed, all because you didn't turn up at the meeting.

FI: I know. That's why I did. (*There is a stunned silence from Charlene and Tracey*)

TRACEY: You did go?

FI: Of course. (*The realisation dawns*) You though I hadn't? You assumed I hadn't.

TRACEY: I'm sorry.

FI: Now isn't that typical of you. You always think the worst of me.

CHARLENE: That's not true, Fi. Tracey's always said how much...

FI: (*Rounding on her*) And you're just as bad. O I've seen the looks you give each other behind my back. You think you're better than me, don't you. You sit in here, in this subterranean hole passing judgement, when you don't know half of what's happening outside in the real world.

TRACEY: The real world! O yes, I wish I lived in the real world.

FI: It's not all bad.

TRACEY: No, happy smiling mums and dads playing with baby in the park.

FI: (*Defensively*) Yes. What's wrong with that?

CHARLENE: Because you know what lies behind the fairy tale pictures Fi, the same as we do. Don't fool yourself.

FI: No, you're fooling yourselves. Why do you think you're so right when hardly anybody agrees with you? You're in a minority.

CHARLENE: Look Fi...

TRACEY: No, let her say it. She should have said all this ages ago. We'd have known where we stood.

FI: I'm going back to the real world.

CHARLENE: You can't go...

TRACEY: O let her go back to Jedsy Wedsy and her cosy wosy little life.

FI: It's not as cosy as you imagine. You don't know what it's like to be manned.

TRACEY: Thank God.

FI: You don't have that kind of strain. It's easier for you.

TRACEY: Easier for me! Pretending I don't exist. Pretending always there's a man in the background. Emerging by night like a rat. Having less right than a rat to exist. Easier for Charlene? She owes her survival to the greed of a few Menace. Easy for us living from hand to mouth...

FI: I bring you all the little luxuries I can spare. Jed doesn't mind a bit...

TRACEY: O thank you master, for the crumbs under your table. We are not worthy. *(She goes on to her knees as though praying)*

FI: You're so unfair. So aggressive. What's Jed supposed to do? He doesn't agree with the Menace. He hates them as much as we do. He suffers under them too.

TRACEY: Ah my heart bleeds.

FI: He feels terribly excluded. He doesn't fit in anywhere. He's under a lot of pressure. He is neutral.

TRACEY: *(Getting to her feet)* Praise the Lord for neutral men. *(She exits)*

CHARLENE: This has all got out of hand, Fi. Tracey doesn't mean you any harm. She wouldn't want to hurt you. Things have been an enormous strain for her. And then to crown it all the patrol paid us a visit last night. I think they suspect about the club...

FI: I'm not interested in your club. I've had enough of you. You're a relic of the past. You're as faded and out of touch as this place.

CHARLENE: Fi, let's just sit down and talk about all this. *(She moves towards Fi)* We'll have some tea.

FI: Don't touch me.

CHARLENE: Alright Fi, alright. Make yourself comfortable. I won't be long. *(She exits)*

FI: *(On her own, mimicking Charlene)* Make yourself comfortable, Fi. Have a cup of tea, Fi. Tea Fi. Tea Fi. *(Turns towards door and shouts abruptly)* Don't want tea, so there, Freak. Gather up my crumbs... Go on, gather up my crumbs. *(She moves restlessly about the room)* Give us this day our daily bread, for thine is the kingdom, the Powerhouse and... *(She looks around her terrified)* For ever and ever. *(She starts to sing)* Polly, put the kettle on, we'll all have tea. *(Suddenly very sober)* No, don't want tea. I don't like it here.

Want to get out. Jed. Jed. Guess who? Three guesses. No, no it's me. No, don't say that, Jed. Of course I'm real. That's not funny. *(She sings quickly her eyes shut)* Polly put the kettle on, we'll all have tea. And toast. Tea 'n toast. Tea 'n toast. Mummy.

CHARLENE: *(Voice off calling to Fi)* I won't be long, Fi.

FI: *(Suddenly alert and panicked)* I bet they're watching. Listening. Ssh. Got to get out of here. *(She starts to put on day clothes to move out of the club)* Got to get back to the real world. *(She giggles)* Mind how you go, Fi. Careful how you go. *(Suddenly terrified)* I bet they've locked the door. I'm trapped in here. I can't breathe, I want to get out. Mummy let me out. Open the door, mummy. *(In her breakdown she sees Charlene as a priest and Tracey as a server carrying the cross moving out to the front of the stage)* Daddy? Ooh sorry. Jed? *(Mumbling to herself)* Never take sweets from a stranger.

SCENE ELEVEN

FI'S BREAKDOWN

(The priest in embroidered robes and the server in a spivy suit with a cross in front of him stand facing out to the audience either side of the stage. Fi cowers in the background)

PRIEST: *(Intoning)* Let us now praise infamous men and their fathers that begat them. Let us give thanks to the Menace. *(They both sing together to the tune of the hymn "praise my soul the king of heaven")*

BOTH: We can all be good and kind men Never raising hand or voice
There are men who do it for us
Secretly we all rejoice
Praise them (x4)
Because of them we have a choice.

(Fi falls on her knees. The priest and server close in on her. She prays quickly and fearfully)

FI: I acknowledge and bewail the manifold sins and wickedness in men and in my own man in particular. The burden of his guilt has been intolerable to me. But we've borne the cross together for so long, working towards the salvation of his soul. It wasn't an easy path. But how can I leave him now? How can I lay me down beside still waters, while he remains in the valley of the shadow of death? What profit I, if I gain the kingdom of heaven and he goes out and becomes a Menace?

(The server hangs the upended cross from the top of the frame and the priest sits and swings to and fro whilst singing. The server is straddled arrogantly across the frame)

PRIEST : Let us give thanks to the Menace.
BOTH : *(Sing)* They put women where we want them
          Ever in a state of fear
          Coming to us for their protection
          Strings attached we make that clear
          Praise them (x4)
          These are men we must revere.

(At the end of the second verse they come forward to sing the third verse up-tempo rugby style with a boisterous knees up)

BOTH : Forgive us if we must condemn them
          For all the times they've raped and killed.
          Their sacrifice has made life smoother,
          Oiled by the blood they've spilled
SERVER : Have a banana.
BOTH : Praise them (x4)
          We are blameless, free from guilt.
PRIEST : Inky pinky parley voo.
BOTH : (Reverent again) A-Menace.

(Server moves towards Fi, backing her across stage to the cage, perhaps dance-like, as he corners her whistling the hymn. Priest meanwhile moves into cage, unseen by Fi. She comes level with cage)

SERVER: Hail, Mary… *(Fi turns to escape and is cornered by the priest)*
PRIEST: The Lord is with thee. *(Fi sinks to her knees on the stool between the server and the priest, in cage/confessional/interrogation centre).*
FI: I confess. I am a miserable sinner.
PRIEST: Lighten our darkness we beseech thee. *(Server snaps on lighter, lights incense stick, then holds lighter under her face)*
FI: I have sinned in thought, word and deed against the Menace.
PRIEST: You will disappear quietly in the night.
SERVER: Disappear in the night. *(Snaps light off abruptly)*
PRIEST: And what else?
FI: I've committed crimes against the Menace.
PRIEST: You may return, though never quite the same.
SERVER: Never quite the same.
PRIEST: What else?

FI: I've conspired to destroy the Powerhouse.

PRIEST: You shall be found with a broken neck.

SERVER: A broken neck. (Server turns her head to one side)

PRIEST: In what other ways have you sinned, O daughter of Eve?

FI: I don't know… I don't think…

SERVER: (Snake-like) Remember your treachery in the garden, O daughter of Eve?

FI: In the garden? O, in the garden…

PRIEST: First breaker of divine law, chained by your sins, henceforth shall you be slave to the master.

SERVER: Obey your master. (Pushes her forward)

PRIEST: What else?

SERVER: She was in league with the devil. She made man fall. (He hisses)

PRIEST: Scourge her body. Only by pain can you atone. What else?

SERVER: (His voice caressing her body viley) She has flesh, breasts, skin, belly, thighs—all to tempt man.

FI: I'm sorry… I'm sorry. Please forgive me.

(Priest and server look at each other and smile. The server goes to collect tray on which is wine, an apple and a high-heeled shoe)

PRIEST: Do you indeed repent ye of your sins and wickedness?

FI: Yes, yes.

PRIEST: Then draw near with faith, and take these sacraments to your discomfort.

FI: (Quickly and thankfully) Give us this day our daily bread and forgive us our trespasses. (She stops suddenly in her tracks) Never take sweets from a stranger? (Looks at them but they are busy with communion, the priest begins it)

PRIEST: Take, eat (Gives apple to server) O daughter of Eve.

SERVER: Take, eat (Holds out apple to Fi) in remembrance of me. (Fi takes a bite. They watch her chew)

PRIEST: Drink this (Priest pours wine into high-heeled show and gives it to server. Server gives it to Fi) the cup of eternal suffering.

SERVER: (With relish) It runneth over. (She takes a gulp as they watch) She's swallowed it.

PRIEST: Yes, it was easy, silly bitch. She's all yours now. You shouldn't have any trouble. (During this exchange Fi spits out chunk of apple and wine. Server turns back to Fi, he has become a fawning shoe shop assistant)

SERVER: Can I help you, Madam? Can anyone help you, Madam?

FI: Yes, I want a comfortable shoe. (Throws down high-heel) Something easy to wear and long-lasting.

SERVER: A shoe with style that takes you miles and makes you smile?

FI: (Pressing on) Something well-fitting and nice looking.

SERVER: *(Lewdly)* Ah, something naughty but nice.

FI: *(Determined)* Something practical, for all occasions.

SERVER: Something with class that'll make you pass. Ankle, knee or thigh?

FI: What do you mean?

SERVER: What do you want? Do you want them for lying, sitting or hobbling?

FI: No, I want to walk in them.

SERVER: *(Put out)* O. I think I've got just the thing madam, what size?

FI: Size five.

SERVER: *(Picks up the high-heel shoe again)* Here we have a saucy little number. Note the cruel heel.

SERVER: *(He bangs the heels into the palms of her hands. She stretches out her arms, christ-like. He bends over to put the shoe on her foot)* I always say the foot's position in the shoe is like the position of the sexual organs during intercourse, don't you agree?

FI: *(Kicking it off)* It doesn't fit.

SERVER: *(Severely)* Fits like a glove, madam. Looks very sexy in a stockinged leg. Beats the pants off trousers.

FI: I just can't get it on.

SERVER: *(Dismayed)* Tut, tut, madam. Have to try another one. Try the leather this time, shall we? *(Sadistic)* With straps and buckles. *(He goes over to the priest who is standing at the mike and whispers to him. They look at her)*

PRIEST: *(Through Tannoy)* Ding dong, shoppers. Bondage on the fifth floor. Women in chains.

FI: *(Sitting up defiantly)* I'm not chained to the kitchen sink. I'm free to do whatever I like. I like whatever I do. I do. *(Pause)* Don't I?

PRIEST: *(Through Tannoy)* Ding dong, slave girls on the seventh floor, shoppers.

FI: I don't slave over a hot stove all day. I buy fast food in disposable containers. Contained. Disposed of. Used once and thrown away. Used once and given the boot. *(Server comes over to her with a boot. She sits upright as he goes down on one knee)*

SERVER: Ready to try another one, madam? Good. *(Renewed confidence)* I'm afraid we've only got them in size three.

FI: Size three? But I think...

SERVER: I think we can get them on at a pinch, madam. *(He pulls and pulls)* At a pinch, madam. Pinch your bum, madam.

FI: Ouch.

SERVER: One two, on with the shoe.

FI: Ouch.

SERVER: Three four, try some more.

FI: Ouch ouch.

SERVER: Five six, it fits it fits. Seven eight...

FI: Wait wait. I want to try another one. *(Server looks helplessly at the priest)*

PRIEST: Ding dong, sado-masochism on the ninth floor. Women beaten, prices slashed.

FI: *(Standing up)* I won't be beaten. *(Stamps foot)* I'm not a doormat. They can't tread the dirt in.

SERVER: *(Nervous now)* These won't show the dirt, madam *(Picks a pair of child's shoes from box)*

FI: But they're tiny. That's a child's shoe.

SERVER: *(On both knees)* Keep your legs crossed, you dirty little girl. Trying it on? Trying it on? Trying it on are you? That's right madam. Trying it on. There. I always say the smallest ones are the snuggest fit.

PRIEST: Ding dong, chicken porn on the twelvth floor. Girls as young and juicy as your daughter.

FI: *(Realisation starting. She pushes her foot into the servers stomach)* Fresh tender young chicken pieces for *their* dinner. Breasts, neck, skin, heart, brains, thighs, legs, stuffed meat.

SERVER: *(Grovelling)* O madam, your feet are like lumps of raw meat. They're deformed. *(Calls out desperately)* Have we got any shoes for ugly, mutilated feet?

PRIEST: Ding dong, snuff movies playing twenty-four hours non-stop. Women strangled and cut up...

FI: No. *(Runs off)* No no no.

SERVER: *(Crawling after her on his belly)* O madam, don't let the boss see you. He's kinky about bare feet. *(Blackout)*

(Lights on with Fi on stage looking at a litter of shoes. Tracey comes on)

FI: Trace, I think I'm in a bit of a mess.

TRACEY: That's alright. Don't worry. We'll sort this lot out. *(Sings as she throws off the garbage of the breakdown scene)*

> This has got to go.
> One two throw
> Nasty little things, chuck 'em out.
> *(Song)*

"BREAKING IT DOWN" SONG

> Was I integrated?
> Totally disintegrating
> Everything's revolving
>
> Spinning, swirling
> Daren't go forward
> Can't go backward

Ready, steady
Don't feel ready
Don't feel steady
Go
Don't want to go
Don't want to know what I know
Don't know what I want

Breaking, breaking down
Breaking, breaking down
Breaking, breaking it down.

I'll stick a pin in your inflatable doll
Stick a pin in your inflated ego
Stick a pin in your inflated ego
Women's bodies, commodities
Take your hands off my body, give it back!

SCENE TWELVE

(Tracey performs the Karate Kata from beginning to end)

SCENE THIRTEEN

CHARLENE'S CLUB

(Charlene enters, carrying a tray of drinks. She gives drinks to Tracey and Fi)

CHARLENE: Ladies, why don't we call this my little celebration.
TRACEY: Yeah, let's have a party.
CHARLENE: It's a little more intimate than the first one I planned…
TRACEY: But just as good.
CHARLENE: And who knows, maybe Sappho will drop in one day.
FI: Who's Sappho?
TRACEY AND CHARLENE: O Fi. *(They both burst out laughing)*
FI: Well, there are so many women. I get them all confused.
CHARLENE: Sappho was one hell of a Greek poet, Fi.
FI: O I remember now. *(She raises her glass to the two of them)* Well, to Sappho. And to the success of the next 'towning', getting into the Central Powerhouse. *(Tracey splutters into her glass. Charlene swings round on them both)*
CHARLENE: Getting into the Central Powerhouse? Did I hear you correctly? You must be crazy.

FI: Charlene we've got to know what's inside. Nothing we've done so far has had any effect. They're just carrying on as usual.

CHARLENE: That's not true and you know it. They've stepped up the guards. Have you two taken that into consideration?

TRACEY: The whole thing's timed exactly. We've got 20 minutes to get in and out.

CHARLENE: What about the guards?

TRACEY: *(Flippantly)* We'll wave to them as we go in. Cooee.

CHARLENE: It's not funny.

TRACEY: Look, don't worry, we are prepared for what we have to do.

CHARLENE: Prepared for what? What does that mean?

FI: Charlene, it is them or us.

CHARLENE: Look, I'm not passing judgement. I don't know whether I'm a pacifist or a coward. I just cannot stand the thought of violence. I could never physically harm anybody.

FI: But suppose Tracey or I were hurt, wouldn't you want to do something?

CHARLENE: I couldn't bear to think about it.

SCENE FOURTEEN

INSIDE CHARLENE'S HEAD THE SHADOWS
OF TERROR MANIFEST THEMSELVES

(The lights fade on all but Charlene who stands alone in this dark light)

CHARLENE: I couldn't bear to think about it. I'd be paralysed with fear. Why can't I get it out of my mind? *(Singing in a low voice)*

> To prepare for violence
> Is so very strange
> My imagination fails me
> Self-defence
> So many doubts about up-front fighting.
> What happens if I miss? You enrage the monster
> Terror, night, street fight.

(Split stage. The light goes off on Charlene and comes up on Fi and Tracey in sparring position, facing the audience, on either side of the stage. Charlene's voice is still heard but she is in darkness. Her voice is a tight, terrified whisper)

CHARLENE: She was alone. It was the night before her wedding, when everyone knew she would be alone. She moved about the deserted house, checking every lock. Down the empty hall her high-heels echoed.

TRACEY: *(As though demonstrating a self-defence lesson, followed by Fi)* Into the shins. Then heel of the hand up into his nose.
CHARLENE: There was a noise from an upstairs room. She had forgotten to lock the bathroom window. Her heart beat wildly beneath her breasts. Her breath came in short gasps.
TRACEY: Breathe, relax and focus. See him, not your fear.
CHARLENE: Her body was rigid with terror. Her throat felt dry and tight.
TRACEY: Straight into the throat with your knuckles.
CHARLENE: She heard his hand turn the door knob. With a moan of fear she sank to her knees.
TRACEY: Kneecaps.
CHARLENE: She looked up to see him towering over her.
TRACEY: Into the groin. Then smash your knee right up into his face.

(The lights fade. When they come up again, Tracey is alone centre stage. On either side two leering masked phantoms are closing in on her. Throughout the following poem Tracey sees the tall figures follow her every movement, watching, photographing her from obscene angles. By the end of the poem her anger is such that she thrusts them aside)

There is a story in the news today
I read it yesterday as well
A woman killed, a child abused
Just another piece of news.
It's nothing new,
It happens this way,
Every hour of every day.

I heard about a man today
Who killed his wife and got away.
Though she was dead, he got away.
She was a nag, the judge advised,
The jury mustn't be surprised.
It's nothing new
It happens this way,
There's no need for explanation.
Just another case of provocation.

Another could not control himself
She was stark naked, after all,
Had flaunted her body shamelessly.
Surprising in a girl of three
Just how seductive she can be.
It's nothing new,

It happens, they say,
There's no need of explanation
Just another case of provocation.

In the scale of rapes it wasn't bad—
Three men and just a little bruising.
She was a bar maid, after all
And no pretence at being a virgin.
Her skirt too short, her blouse too thin
She was dressed to kill, dressed to provoke.
It's nothing new,
It happens this way,
Every hour of every day.

If in the coming days you read
The news of some appalling crime—
A rapist in an alleyway,
Disarmed and bleeding, left for dead,
Don't be alarmed—it's nothing new,
Just the old familiar rage.
And one more case of provocation.

(Fi is at one side of the stage in darkness. On the other side of the stage is Charlene in a dark pin-point of light. A rhythmic guitar accompanies the voices and builds in intensity)

FI'S VOICE: Suppose Tracey or I were hurt, wouldn't you want to do something?

CHARLENE: I couldn't bear to think about it. Why can't I get it out of my mind? Anything could happen to her.

FI'S VOICE: We were outside the Powerhouse waiting for the all-clear when the guard saw us. Tracey was taken.

CHARLENE: Anything could happen to her.

FI'S VOICE: As we went through the doors, the alarm went off, Tracey was shot.

CHARLENE: Anything could happen to her.

FI'S VOICE: The door was electrified, she didn't stand a chance.

CHARLENE: Anything could happen to her.

FI'S VOICE: We never got to the Powerhouse. I got through the Control Point but they knew Tracey's pass was forged. She was taken.

CHARLENE: Disappeared like all the other women. *(In the background music is heard, soft but relentless and driving)*

FI'S VOICE: *(Reading off the names of women killed or persecuted for their resistance)* Petronella de Meath, Maria Miguel, Ingird Roheim, Sonja Hendrikson.

CHARLENE: Every hour of every day.

FI'S VOICE: Louise Noel, Euginie Lillie, Anna Celestina, Nina Conté

CHARLENE: I feed the old familiar range.

FI'S VOICE: Agnes Samson, Jilly Duncan, Moira Kent, Bridget Cleary

CHARLENE: How do I know my strength till I prove it? Strength does not come by doing nothing. I cannot do nothing. (*Other instruments join the guitar, building into the last song*)

SELF DEFENSE

> To prepare for violence
> Is so very strange
> My imagination fails me
> Self-defense
> So many doubts about up-front fighting
> What happens if I miss
> You enrage the monster
> Terror, night, street, fight, then!

CHORUS
> Fist fight
> Fight back
> To fight back is not so easy
> Fist fight
> Jam tight
> To fight back is not so easy
> To fight back is not so easy

> Woman unsure, foot sore
> Going home alone
> A woman and it's midnight
> I'm worn to the bone
> Shadows before my eyes
> Trees like people
> They terrorise me
> Late night I'm on my own
> To fight back is not so easy
> Imagination fills in for life
> My mind has learned to kill
> Yes my mind has learned to kill

CHORUS
> Not quite the end

(Back in the matriarchal computer centre the projection of the future fades)

ALL: It's REWOP, that's what's in their Powerhouse!

COMPUTER: They stole REWOP and reversed it to make power! Just let me get my electrodes into them…

OCTAVE: O dear.

TREBLE: How far into the future would all this be?

COMPUTER: Can't tell.

TREBLE: You mean it could be 50 years or 5,000 years?

COMPUTER: 5 million. I haven't got a chronology meter in my chip. The newer models now…

OCTAVE: It is only a possible projection remember.

TREBLE: But we must do something, even so.

OCTAVE: We'll call an emergency general meeting immediately.

TREBLE: Not yet. We mustn't introduce panic. Let's just think of some possible alternatives for action to suggest to the sisters.

OCTAVE: Well, presumably the men took the extreme step of stealing REWOP because they felt left out of everything. Perhaps if we encourage them a bit…

TREBLE: Nonsense, involve them in high technology! They've never shown the slightest degree of interest. Besides, they're tone deaf.

COMPUTER: Lot of money to be made in computers…

TREBLE: What! Who told you that? O, as if I didn't know. You see, Octave, the men are already exerting a bad influence on our machines.

OCTAVE: But if each of us sort of fostered one man, perhaps we could have a good influence over them.

TREBLE: Hmm. What do you think, computer? Divide and influence them for the good.

COMPUTER: A possible solution, but they reverse everything, remember. So you could end up being divided and influenced by them. For the worst.

TREBLE: On the other hand, we could divide the planet in two, and bar the men from our half.

OCTAVE: But then we wouldn't know what they were up to on their side.

COMPUTER: You could always reduce their influence by zero male birthrate.

TREBLE
OCTAVE TOGETHER: Zero male population growth!

COMPUTER: Still, it's up to you. I am only the computer after all. It doesn't matter to me. We hope you are comfortable. Have a nice trip now.

THE END

Curfew. Jude Winter (Wonder Woman). Photo: Anita Corbin.

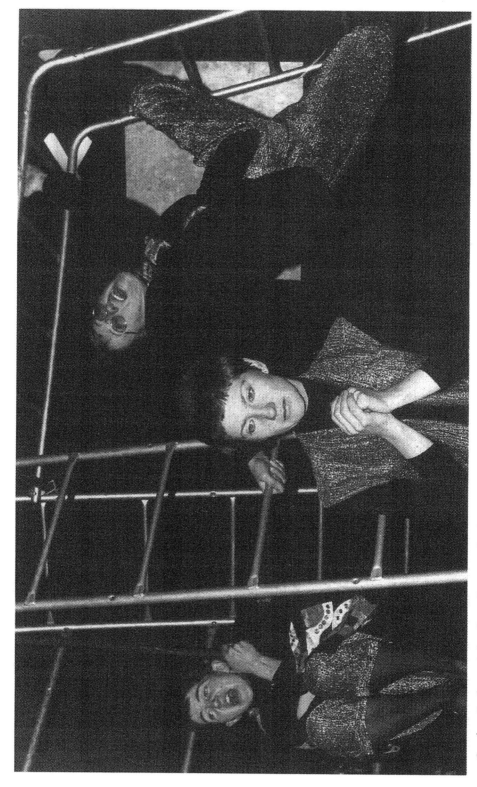

Curfew. Left to right: Jane Boston, Jude Winter and Tasha Fairbanks. Photo: Dianne Ceresa.

PULP

by
TASHA FAIRBANKS

FROM DISCUSSION AND WORKSHOPS WITH SIREN THEATRE
COMPANY

SONG LYRICS: JANE BOSTON
COMPOSITION: JANE BOSTON AND JUDE WINTER

FIRST PERFORMED AT THE DRILL HALL, LONDON, 1985

THE COMPANY

MAGDA AND DAGMAR: JANE BOSTON
HEDDY AND ELLA: JUDE WINTER
DOLORES AND MONIKA: TASHA FAIRBANKS
KAY: HILARY RAMSDEN

DESIGNER AND TECHNICIAN: DEBRA TRETHEWEY

THE PLAY WAS DIRECTED BY NOELLE JANACZEWSKA

PERFORMANCE NOTES

There are two time dimensions in PULP. The bulk of the action takes place in a sleazy downtown New York bar, during the McCarthyite Fifties, and is set over a period of several months. Another, parallel, story is set in Ella's up-market London flat, in 1985, during the course of one evening.

Magda and Dagmar are one woman, living in two different time zones, both unaware of each other.

THE FIFTIES CHARACTERS

Magda—Early thirties. At the opening of the play she is a beautiful, glamorous Hollywood star, at the height of her profession, but about to topple.
Heddy—Mid-thirties. A journalist with a social conscience.
Kay—Mid-thirties. An apparently inept private eye.
Dolores—Early twenties. A dangerously ambitious dreamer.

THE EIGHTIES CHARACTERS

Dagmar—Late twenties. An employee in a British Government security service. She is played by the same actor who plays Magda.
Ella—Early forties. A senior employee in the same service and Dagmar's lover.
Monika—Mid-fifties. Ella's next-door-neighbour and a German expatriate.

STAGE DESIGN

The stage was divided into Fifties New York, represented by a period drinks bar, lit garishly from inside and padded with orange leopard skin. Around were a few high stools. The Eighties side was represented by a couple of sterile-looking designer armchairs and a coffee table. Behind both areas were tall flats, padded in black velvet.

The lighting aimed at a 'film noir' effect, contained and directional, producing stark light and shadow.

THE MUSIC

Because of Magda's role as a bar room singer, much of the music in this play was able to emerge fairly seamlessly out of the action, (i.e. with 'Trouble', 'Time' and 'Looking at Lana'), once an audience had become accustomed to the other actors dropping their roles and picking up rock instruments.

'Trouble' served as a narrative device to install Magda in the club and convey time passing; 'Time' set an atmosphere for type dislocation of reality in the piece; 'Looking at Lana' echoed the nostalgic longing of Heddy for her 'great Hollywood dream'; and 'Pulp' framed the opening of the play with a lyrical foretelling of what is to come.

Of the song and dance routines, 'Dance with a Difference' was a joyous and funny moment of togetherness for the four women, before betrayal divided them. 'Odd Girl Out' was a sinister presentiment of danger for the spies who are spied upon.

PULP

Pulp Song

ACT ONE
SCENE ONE

HEDDY: A seedy tale, told on seedy paper. But one that's got to be told if only to understand. That's important. It's important to get things straight, that you see why things happened like they did. I've always thought of myself kind of outside of things. Detached—an observer of other people's lives. That's how it started out. And that's how it should've gone on. But somehow, somewhere along the line, I got involved in the whole messy business. I can't even say when exactly. One minute I was propping up the bar, lapping up the action, smiling inside—and the next thing I knew I was in up to my neck.

It shouldn't have been like that. As a reporter you deal in facts, pure and simple. Well, that's how I saw it. I've learned a lot since then. Like, facts aren't pure or simple. It's what people do with them that matters.

Yeah, O.K., I should've known better. Should've seen earlier. But I wanted to get to the truth. It was too late when I realised truth comes in a lot of different forms, and it all depends on who's looking at it and from where. Maybe if I'd thought this out sooner, a lot of what happened could have been avoided.

But I'm getting ahead of myself. It all started... when? I guess you can't ever say when something really began. Or when, if ever, it ends. But for the sake of the records, let's say this story dates from July 5th 1955, exactly six months ago. It all started with old Joe McCarthy and his gang of commie bashers. Joe McCarthy was worried that Joe Stalin had got himself some pals in the movie industry. He thought Hollywood might start shooting propaganda pictures against Uncle Sam and Momma's home-made apple pie. So he started the biggest witch-hunt since the Spanish Inquisition. Anyone who'd ever put a dime into a Civil Rights collecting box suddenly got a file on her an inch thick. With the risk of losing their swimming pools along with their reputations, the Hollywood greats fell over themselves to co-operate with Joe—McCarthy, that is. In 1955 Judas would have had himself one heck of a time in Beverley Hills.

Well, anyway, that's how come Clara Lamont was found that night in the bath of her home in Sunset Boulevard, with her wrists slashed and her stomach full of gin and phenobarbitone.

(Black-out. Lights up on Magda alone in spot)

41

ACT ONE
SCENE TWO

VOICE: Miss Thornton, the House Committee for Un-American activities would like to thank you for your extreme honesty and candour in co-operating with us. You have proved a very friendly witness, and have given us all the information required. Thank you. (*Black-out and cameras popping. Magda moves away*)
MAGDA: No comment. No comment.

ACT ONE
SCENE THREE

(*Lights come up on Magda with her back to audience, retching, while Heddy casually watches her*)

HEDDY: Like fishbones, aren't they?
MAGDA: (*Spinning round*) What?
HEDDY: Lies. Like fishbones. They stick in your throat.
MAGDA: What the hell are you talking about?
HEDDY: Nice little performance you gave at the Hearing. Probably your best. Shame Sam Goldwyn didn't catch it on celluloid.
MAGDA: Who the hell are you?
HEDDY: Heddy Vance, reporter. (*Flashes card*) New York Chronicle.
MAGDA: Press! I said 'no comment' and I meant 'no comment'. Get it?
HEDDY: Sure. You know, it's a funny thing being a woman in this game. The guys go into the Men's Room and come out with a story. You'd never believe how much business gets done in the Men's Room. Now I've got a disadvantage there.
MAGDA: And you thought this would be your big chance? So you followed me in here thinking you'd get yourself a story. Forget it.
HEDDY: No, you wouldn't even rate a paragraph. So you spill the beans on all your friends, maybe even make up a few stories to please the Committee...
MAGDA: Now listen you...
HEDDY: I said 'maybe'. But that's not news any more. Nowadays everyone who gets in that box just suddenly can't stop talking. The things they know for an absolute fact about their best friends would amaze... even their best friends.
MAGDA: So I'm nothing special. Go waste your time elsewhere.
HEDDY: No, what you did won't make a story.
MAGDA: What a pity for you.
HEDDY: Me? O, don't worry about me. I'll live. Unlike your... room-mate, Clara Lamont.

MAGDA: Get out. Get out, do you hear? Leave me alone.

HEDDY: Now, on the other hand, if you'd told McCarthy and the boys they were a cheap bunch of opportunists advancing their own careers by ruining people's lives—now that would have been a story, Miss Thornton.

MAGDA: And lost me my contract with the studios, thank you. I don't go in for heroics in real life, Miss...

HEDDY: Vance. Mm, funny people, movie tycoons. Like to keep their hands nice and antiseptic. I wonder if they're thinking you're not a little too dangerous to know right now.

MAGDA: I was cleared completely. And I did my duty as an American citizen.

HEDDY: Sure, sure, but you can't step in shit and come out clean.

MAGDA: What do you mean?

HEDDY: Being connected with suicide—makes people... edgy. And anyway, 'guilt by association'. You knew her... very well, didn't you?

MAGDA: Not all that well, I shared her house for a while. Look, I don't know what this has got to do with you, or what the hell you're insinuating...

HEDDY: Sure you do. You know damn well. I bet you a nickel to a long cool beer, Universal Studios are having second thoughts about Magda Thornton right now.

(Black-out)

ACT ONE
SCENE FOUR

(Magda in spot on her own)

MAGDA: Hello. Get me Mr. Goldwyn. It's Magda Thornton here. No, I never speak to secretaries. Hello, Sam, it's Magda... what do you mean recasting?

(Black-out)

ACT ONE
SCENE FIVE

(Lights up on Heddy & Magda in bar)

MAGDA: Why have you brought me here?

HEDDY: No one asks your business. Why should they? Everyone here's got something to hide.

MAGDA: O.K. So what's your game? If it's not a story, where's the catch?

HEDDY: No catch.

MAGDA: Don't give me that one. I've been around too long. Nobody gives something for nothing. There's always a catch.

HEDDY: Just think of me as a fellow-traveller.

MAGDA: I don't get you.

HEDDY: Miss Thornton, I've always deeply admired you. Magda Thornton, what an actress—no one could touch her. Especially not a man.

MAGDA: So it's blackmail. Just get your arse out of my sight…

HEDDY: Miss Thornton, I'm sorry to labour the point, but you're not even worth blackmailing. So who's interested in the sex-life of Magda Thornton nobody?

MAGDA: Now just you listen, and listen good. For the moment things aren't looking too hot for me. O.K. But once this business has blown over, and it will, don't worry, all I'll have to do is snap my fingers and every studio in Hollywood'll be falling over themselves to sign me up. And you know why? Because I am Magda Thornton somebody. I have a following that stretches from Broadway to every hick, one horse town in New Mexico. *(Rising)* But thank you for the drink, and the pearls of… unwanted wisdom.

HEDDY: My pleasure. By the way, you'll be in need of a job. I know the guy who runs this joint. Name of Victor. He's looking for a singer.

MAGDA: I'll treat that suggestion with the contempt it deserves. Goodbye, Miss…

HEDDY: Vance. Heddy Vance. My card.

MAGDA: Don't waste it on me, sweetheart. I'll never have occasion to use it.

HEDDY: Maybe. Take it anyway. You never know. Two, three weeks in line on a soup kitchen, sleeping rough on 42nd, and Victor's going to look as pretty as Mr. Ziegfeld.

(Black-out)

ACT ONE
SCENE SIX

(Spot up on Magda singing in the bar) (Trouble song)

ACT ONE
SCENE SEVEN

DOLORES: *(At the end of the song)* That was breathtaking. You have the most mellifluous voice.

MAGDA: I have what?

DOLORES: O, I guess I don't pronounce it right. I've only ever read it in books. I meant you sing beautifully.

MAGDA: Why thank you, Dolores. That's kind of you to say so.

DOLORES: I take singing lessons twice a week. But I'll never be anything like you, Magda. I guess I'll spend my life waiting tables. *(Pause)* You know, Magda, this may seem kind of strange, but every time I look at you I think of a famous movie star.

MAGDA: *(Sharply)* Who?

DOLORES: Why, Lana Hope, of course. She's my idol. Victor's got a picture of her in his office. I don't like that. I hate to think of him ogling over her.

MAGDA: Lana Hope?

DOLORES: You must have heard of her. She was in all the old pictures. I only ever go see old movies. That's where I feel at home. You ever get that feeling, Magda? Like you belong to another time, and that's where you should really be? Sometimes I have this real crazy feeling there's another me living in those old movies.

MAGDA: You never look at a newspaper, Dolores?

DOLORES: Not since I got to New York. Back in Arkansas we got the Harrisville Post. Local gossip, you know. Small town stuff. Who'd bought a new mobile home, or had a barbecue party.

MAGDA: Sounds kind of homey.

DOLORES: Trouble was everyone knew your business. I guess it's O.K. if you're like them.

MAGDA: You were a bit wild for Harrisville, huh?

DOLORES: I... I just didn't fit in.

MAGDA: And how do you like the big city, where no one knows you, and nobody gives a damn?

DOLORES: At least no one here points a finger.

MAGDA: *(Abruptly)* You'd better go. Victor will be wondering where you are.

DOLORES: Only because he wants to start pawing me again.

MAGDA: Is Victor doing that?

DOLORES: He tries.

MAGDA: And you don't want it?

DOLORES: Hell, no.

MAGDA: Just a question. Some girls don't mind it. They reckon it'll get them promotion, or a pay rise. Some like it. He's not bad looking.

DOLORES: I'm not like that. I'm not like that at all. He makes me feel sick. Always getting me to come into his office on some pretext. Then his face goes all loose and he starts breathing heavy.

MAGDA: You should have told me before. I'll have a little word with Victor about it. He won't do it again.

DOLORES: O thank you.

MAGDA: *(Laughs)* No problem.

DOLORES: Magda, I don't have any friends. I'd like to think of you as my friend. Can I?

MAGDA: Why sure you can.

DOLORES: O, that makes me feel so good. I think any friend of yours must be real lucky. *(Exits)*

MAGDA: *(To herself)* O Clara. If there is a me living another life out there. I just hope to God I'm doing better…

(Black- out)

ACT ONE
SCENE EIGHT

(London. A Sunday afternoon in Ella's expensive flat)

ELLA: Dagmar, what exactly did you say to my mother in this drunken exchange of confidence?

DAGMAR: I just said men and women were intrinsically unsuited together.

ELLA: You said what?!

DAGMAR: I said men were really much happier in each other's company. It brings out the qualities they most admire. Like camaraderie, putting on terribly brave fronts, and dying in each other's arms.

ELLA: O God.

DAGMAR: And it left women free to have a good time too.

ELLA: You said that to my mother?

DAGMAR: Yes. She agreed with me.

ELLA: I don't believe you. My mother comes from a long line of dog breeders and Parish Councillors.

DAGMAR: Mind you, she was onto her fourth Martini by then. She won't remember a thing tomorrow. She was for too tipsy.

ELLA: I know, that's the only reason I haven't wrung your neck.

DAGMAR: O come on. This is 1985. We have had Women's Liberation. God rest its soul! Anyway, I never once mentioned the dreaded word.

ELLA: Am I supposed to be grateful for that small mercy?

DAGMAR: It dared not speak its name.

ELLA: Dagmar, all this playing at being visible might seem clever to you, but it's actually extremely irritating and immature.

DAGMAR: And if I'm not 'playing' at it?

ELLA: You wouldn't stay five minutes in the Department. Don't be ridiculous.

DAGMAR: In an establishment renowned for its double dealing and dirty tricks, you'd think a few perverts could be easily assimilated.

ELLA: Dagmar.

DAGMAR: Well, why not?

ELLA: You know very well why not. For one thing, you'd be an enormous security risk.

DAGMAR: And for another?

ELLA: You'd be incriminating me, you damn fool. Do you imagine I'd allow that?

(Black-out)

ACT ONE
SCENE NINE

(New York. Heddy is sitting in the bar. Kay sidles in, trying to look inconspicuous, but only managing to look highly suspicious. She looks around the bar. Heddy watches her in amusement.)

HEDDY: Criminals beware. It's Kay Masters, scourge of the underworld.

KAY: Ssshhh, for Chrissakes! Back off, will you. I'm on a job. I'm blending into the background.

HEDDY: Yeah, about as much as a giraffe would. Sit down. You won't look so conspicuous. *(Kay rakes the bar clients with her eyes)* Something I should know about?

KAY: Uh uh. Routine case. Dame took a powder, left her old man. Back in Arkansas. Between you and me I don't blame her. He reckons she's hit town. *(Takes out a photo)*

HEDDY: *(Picking up photo)* This her? *(She starts in surprise)*

KAY: Yep, seen her around?

(Dolores comes up to take the order Kay is looking down, fumbling with something in her bag)

DOLORES: Want something to drink?

(Heddy surreptitiously shows the photo to Dolores, who gasps and shrinks back, terrified)

HEDDY: Never seen her in my life.

KAY: *(To Dolores, without looking up)* Not for me, sister. *(Dolores backs right off)* Today I covered every bar in the Bronx. Do you know how many bars there are in the Bronx? I'm so full of sasparilla, I could bust.

HEDDY: Why don't you drink rye, like any self-respecting detective?

KAY: Rye rots your guts.

HEDDY: Sasparilla rots your teeth, what's the difference?

KAY: Hey, that singer, know who she is? Magda Thornton. Yeah, I pride myself on noticing everything. Eyes and ears always open, that's the secret. Remember that and you'll be a good journalist some day.

HEDDY: Thanks for the tip. So, "on to the next whisky bar".

KAY: My feet are sore. You know, she sings good. Maybe I will have that sasparilla after all.

HEDDY: The sasparilla here is terrible.

KAY: Everywhere the sasparilla's terrible. I like the singer.

HEDDY: You like the singer? I'll bring her over. Stay there. Don't move.

KAY: You want I should put my hands up, too? And tell that waitress to come back. I want a sas ...

HEDDY: No, you don't. Think of your dentist bills.

(Black-out)

ACT ONE
SCENE TEN

(In Victor's office immediately after)

DOLORES: Magda, I can't go back. I just couldn't bear it. I'd rather kill myself.

MAGDA: (Violently) Shut up, you fool. Don't talk about killing yourself. (More gently) I'm sorry. It's O.K., Dolores. It's O.K.

DOLORES: You don't know what Harrisville is like. You don't know what they do to people there. The way they look at you...

MAGDA: Looks don't hurt anybody.

DOLORES: And they whisper behind their hands. Lies. Lies can hurt, Magda, you know that?

MAGDA: Yes, yes, I know that.

DOLORES: And even when it isn't really lies, the things they whisper about you—because of how they say it, the dirty way they're thinking about it—it isn't the truth. Not really. Do you understand what I'm saying, Magda?

MAGDA: I understand.

DOLORES: I had a sister. She used to talk a lot. About women, socialism, stuff like that. Crazy things they said. They used to stare at her real strange. But, you know, she didn't care one bit. Not (Snaps fingers) that much. She just went on talking. So they took her away and they gave her an operation. She didn't talk much after that. She would just stare at you real strange. I don't ever want to go back there, Magda.

MAGDA: You'll never have to

DOLORES: But if Bill knew where I was ...

MAGDA: New York's a big city, Dolores. There are lots of places you can go.

DOLORES: Go? But I couldn't go away from here. I couldn't leave you, Magda. Not now. Not after what's happened. I mean, I thought you and me ... well, isn't it the same for you?

MAGDA: Yes, of course it is. It's the same for me. Now you run along. I'll think of something.

HEDDY: *(Emerging from the shadows)* Might I suggest a solution?

MAGDA: Do you always lurk in doorways?

HEDDY: It's as good a way as any to pick up news.

MAGDA: And a sock in the jaw, if you're not careful.

HEDDY: Want to hear my suggestion?

MAGDA: Spill it.

HEDDY: Our sleuth friend out there will get a little bonus from the husband should she find Dolores. Now I guess she wouldn't be too choosey as to where that bonus came from. With me?

MAGDA: Right alongside. Not one to let ethics get in her way, eh?

HEDDY: Let's just say she has no stakes in the institution of Holy Matrimony.

MAGDA: Yet another one of the sisterhood!

HEDDY: She seems taken by you.

MAGDA: Try not to sound overly surprised. No matter what *you* think of me, some people still are, you know.

HEDDY: *(Looking after Dolores)* So I see.

MAGDA: She's a nice kid.

HEDDY: Hardly your type.

MAGDA: Hardly your business. And I'm not looking for approval from you.

HEDDY: Good. Because you wouldn't get it. Magda, just don't use her, that's all.

MAGDA: Use her? God damn you, I'm trying to help her.

HEDDY: Don't pretend you don't know what I mean. Use her. To appease the gods, your conscience, whatever. I don't know what there is between the two of you, and if you want my opinion...

MAGDA: I don't.

HEDDY: O.K. But whatever you and Dolores have together, leave Clara Lamont out of it.

MAGDA: This may seem strange to your sordid little mind, but I've got news for you—I love Dolores. Want to write it down?

HEDDY: Nope, sorry Magda. I've got my professional reputation to think of. I only print the truth.

(Black-out)

ACT ONE
SCENE ELEVEN

(Back in the bar immediately after. Madga has come to Kay's table)

KAY: Miss Thornton, this is a great pleasure, believe me. *(She gets up and moves what was Heddy's chair round for Madga)*

MAGDA: *(Sitting down)* Call me Madga.

KAY: *(Seeing Heddy now doesn't have a chair she moves her own round for Heddy)* I can't tell you how much I appreciate your coming over here. *(Heddy sits)*

MAGDA: *(Impatiently)* Won't you sit down, Miss...

KAY: Masters. *(Unable to find a chair she lowers herself and crouches uncomfortably at their level)* Kay Masters.

MAGDA: Miss Masters...

KAY: Oh-oh. *(She is waggling her nose furiously)*

MAGDA: What's the matter?

KAY: Itch.

MAGDA: Well, scratch it.

KAY: Uh uh, it's right way down in my sinuses.

MAGDA: Well, can't you just ignore it for the moment.

KAY: O no. The one thing you should never do is ignore it.

HEDDY: Kay, for God's sake. *(The music is heard starting up)*

MAGDA: *(To Heddy)* Lana's theme.

HEDDY: What?

MAGDA: *(To Heddy)* That's what Dolores calls it. *(To Kay)* They're playing my introduction. I don't have much time.

KAY: That's too bad.

MAGDA: I understand you're looking for someone. What's it worth not to find her?

KAY: Not to find her?

MAGDA: Just as a matter of interest, you understand.

KAY: I think I'm beginning to. And, just as a matter of interest, is there perhaps a certain party who may have certain interests in this?

MAGDA: There might be an interested party, yes.

KAY: And, again strictly out of interest, would it be in the interest of this interested party that the whereabouts of this other party remains not established?

MAGDA: I think you've understood the interest of the party concerned correctly.

KAY: For you, Miss Thornton, or rather for the interested party who is apparently interested in the non-whereabouts of the missing person, I think we can safely say she just cannot be found.

MAGDA: How much?

KAY: For you, Miss Thornton, or rather for…

MAGDA: No, no, not that again.

KAY: Nothing.

MAGDA: *(Rising)* It's been a pleasure doing business with you.

KAY: The trouble is, you give me the itch.

MAGDA: That's a very frank proposition, Miss Masters. I don't think I've ever been approached in quite that way before. But I'll be equally frank with you. I'm already involved with someone.

KAY: Huh? O no. My itch. Here. *(She scratches her nose vigourously)* Sign of danger. It's never let me down yet.

MAGDA: *(Looking sharply at Heddy)* Let's hope this will be the first time.

KAY: Anyway, as far as I'm concerned, the case is closed. If she's a friend of yours *(Tears photo in two)* Dolores Selzman no longer exists. *(Magda stares and hurries off)*

HEDDY: Thus spake the prophet.

KAY: *(Rubbing her nose)* But this little baby doesn't lie. You want to know something? That dame spells trouble.

(Black-out)

ACT ONE
SCENE TWELVE

(New York. Few weeks later in the bar after closing time)

DOLORES: You spend a lot of time with Victor.

MAGDA: Do I?

DOLORES: Why's that?

MAGDA: I have a good business head. He appreciates that.

DOLORES: That's not all he appreciates. I've seen him looking at you. He's always watching you.

MAGDA: It would appear he's not the only one.

DOLORES: I know what he's thinking, and I don't like it.

MAGDA: I guess a person's thoughts are free. That's one thing we're all entitled to.

DOLORES: He keeps dirty pictures in his desk drawer.

MAGDA: How do you know what's in his desk? Have you been snooping?

DOLORES: No, of course not. I was just looking for something one day. They're pictures of naked women.

MAGDA: Sounds like Victor.

DOLORES: Women together. He gets off on that. I know, because he's asked me questions about you and me.

MAGDA: Just tell him to go jerk off.

DOLORES: It's the most beautiful thing in the world, what we have. But through his eyes it all comes out dirty. I hate him for making me feel like that. When he looks at me and you and thinks those things I could kill him.

MAGDA: Just don't think about it, Dolores. We feel good about what we're doing. That's the important thing.

DOLORES: You know, it matters so much that you feel good about it. Not just about me, but about what we are. The girl I... knew back home made me feel so guilty all the time. She'd say I was sick.

MAGDA: *You* were sick?

DOLORES: Yeah.

MAGDA: And she wasn't? Even though she was one half of it?

DOLORES: She said she really cared about me, but that she never got aroused.

MAGDA: And didn't she?

DOLORES: Well, if not, she was damn good at faking it. *(They laugh)*

MAGDA: And you were so butch and overpowering she couldn't say 'no'.

DOLORES: *(Laughs)* Put like that it sounds so stupid. But at the time I believed her. I felt so bad. Like I was giving her the plague.

MAGDA: Look out Harrisville—here comes a one-woman epidemic! What's she doing now?

DOLORES: Married, two kids. But *(Mischievously)*, you know, I hear she goes two, three times a week to the hairdressers—and always after hours.

MAGDA: She must have the shortest hair in Harrisville.

DOLORES: Yeah. Sure hope she doesn't get taken for a duke. *(Pulls her up gently)* Come on.

MAGDA: Where are you taking me?

DOLORES: To the hairdressers!

(Black-out)

ACT ONE
SCENE THIRTEEN

(London. Sunday afternoon, in Ella's flat)

DAGMAR: We spend half our lives uncovering other people's nasty little secrets, and the other half hiding our own.

ELLA: And are well paid for it. You knew what you were in for when you joined the service.

DAGMAR: I never realised the disgust I would feel when I see our respectable colleagues parading their bed partners and their brattish offspring at parties and I know I can't even touch you in front of them.

ELLA: I can assure you I wouldn't want you to, anyway. I find any public displays of affection extremely distasteful. What we do, we do in private.

DAGMAR: Of course, I'm forgetting my place. I'm for the bedroom only.

ELLA: *(Moving towards her)* I haven't heard you complain about what can be achieved there. Perhaps we should adjourn to it.

DAGMAR: Out of fear, we live bounded by four walls the moments that have any relevance to us.

ELLA: What the hell do you want? Marriage, a semi, and our names on the car windscreen?

DAGMAR: For the office records, no doubt in your Department file, you have a steady relationship with John Huntley, eligible bachelor.

ELLA: *(Seductive)* I don't want to *talk* right now.

DAGMAR: How long before that cover blows? Before he starts telling everyone you're a frigid bitch—or worse. Because you're not succumbing to his irresistable embraces? *(Ella draws back)* Or do you? For the records?

(Black-out)

ACT ONE
SCENE FOURTEEN

(Kay and Heddy are reading the papers in the bar)

HEDDY: Hmm, trouble between the families, I see, Cordoni and some of his boys been gunned down, outside a dive a few blocks from here.

KAY: Cordoni, huh?

HEDDY: Know him?

KAY: Victor married his sister. Then played around some. Cordoni never forgave him. Now I wonder who put a contract out on him? And why?

HEDDY: The usual? Little disagreement about who controls what.

KAY: I heard on the grapevine there's something big coming up. No one seems to know what.

HEDDY: We could always call up the Mayor of Chicago and ask.

KAY: Or the Police Department. They're sure to know what's going to happen.

HEDDY: And be absolutely amazed when it does. *(They laugh and go on reading)* Well, how about that. Pedroza, known South American revolutionary leader rumoured to be in New York. I wouldn't be in that guy's shoes once the C.I.A. get to him.

(Dolores enters with a sweep, looking very dressed up and glam)

HEDDY: Hi, how's the birthday girl?

DOLORES: Fine. Everything's ready. We're just waiting for Magda. She's on her last number.

KAY: *(Getting up)* She is? O, I want to catch it. *(Exits)*

HEDDY: You're looking good.

DOLORES: As good as Lana Hope? *(She poses)*

HEDDY: Well…

DOLORES: Don't worry, you're under no obligation to answer that. Only one woman could ever really play Lana, and that's Magda.

HEDDY: Who's talking about playing her, anyway?

DOLORES: Hollywood. They're making a movie about her.

HEDDY: Poor Lana.

DOLORES: *(Shows Heddy her magazine)* It's right here in Silver Screen, see? They're auditioning now. Magda would be wonderful, wouldn't she? Heddy, wouldn't she just be superb? She would receive the accolades she truly deserves. That is how you say it, isn't it? *(Savours the word)* Accolades.

HEDDY: I wouldn't know. I've never had occasion to use it.

DOLORES: O, that's a shame. Because it doesn't just mean awards and beautiful bouquets, you know. It means people's hearts.

HEDDY: And what does Magda think? Have you shown her this yet?

DOLORES: *(Snatching magazine away)* O no, Magda must never see it. She must never know about this.

HEDDY: I thought you wanted to see her as Lana.

DOLORES: O, I can dream well enough about how it would be, that will suffice. But if she really went to Hollywood, they'd see straight away that she's Lana. I'd lose her forever.

HEDDY: Come on, Dolores, look at the facts. Aren't you over-dramatising just a little? She wouldn't stand a chance amongst a couple of hundred Hollywood starlets, all acting their butts off. O.K., so she can entertain a bar full of misfits and city dregs, but Magda…

DOLORES: Was a star. Magda Thornton.

HEDDY: You knew that?

DOLORES: *(Superior smile)* Of course I know. Magda thinks I don't. That's why I'm so important to her. Because, with me, she has no past. She thinks I don't realise she was once a star. For me she always will be. That's why I can't allow her to go back to Hollywood.

HEDDY: You can't stop her.

DOLORES: O I can. I have to. It would be the end of me otherwise.

HEDDY: Listen, Dolores, you're putting too much onto Magda. It can't work. Sooner or later things'll just explode in your face.

DOLORES: O no. I've thought it all out very carefully. I've made plans for us. She doesn't know it, but I have.

HEDDY: Magda does what she wants.

DOLORES: She thinks she does. But you know, the first time we were... together, she thought it was all her idea. That she seduced me. But I'd already written her the script. All I had to do was feed her the cues.

HEDDY: Dolores. You can't make someone into what you want her to be.

DOLORES: Don't you think she's made me into what she wants? While she's with me, she can forget what she did to Clara Lamont. I give her daily absolution.

HEDDY: You're both playing a dangerous game.

DOLORES: So, it's dangerous. Before I had nothing. All my life I spent looking for Lana. Now I've found her, I won't let her go.

(Black-out)

ACT ONE
SCENE FIFTEEN

(New York. The bar, after closing. It's Dolores' birthday party. They are all laughing and drinking)

KAY: Having observed you all for some time now, I have reached a brilliant deduction.

DOLORES: You have? What's that? Tell us, Kay.

KAY: I deduce we have all one thing in common.

HEDDY: You don't say.

KAY: We are all very drunk.

HEDDY: Sshh, don't tell anyone. It might be Un-American.

(Magda produces a birthday cake)

MAGDA: Let's light the candles.

KAY: *(Lighting a match to them)* I'll do that. Get ready to blow, Dolores. *(Having lighted candles, she blows out match, extinguishing half the candles at the same time. Laughter)*

DOLORES: I didn't even get to make a wish.

KAY: Uh? Did I do that?

HEDDY: Speech. Speech.

KAY: Oh. O.K. Well...

HEDDY: Not you, you fool. Dolores.

DOLORES: O no, I can't Magda...

MAGDA: Go on.

DOLORES: Hmm, hmm. *(Poses theatrically, as though at the oscars)* Darlings... *(Laughter)* I'd just like to say, I love you all. *(Becomes more extravagant, more laughter)* I feel like we're all part of one, big happy family. *(Becoming more serious, but still drunk and giggly)* No, seriously, I do, I do. I feel we're more family than a real family... than my proper... *(Poshly)* ever so pwoper family... *(Laughter)* in whose... to whose reluctant bosom I was born into...

KAY: *(With the bottle of bourbon)* I do solemnly rebaptise you with this holy spirit. *(Pours some over her head)*

DOLORES: Now Magda. And Heddy. Do it to everyone. Go on, *(Kay does, to more laughter)* That's right.

(The Melee takes shape into a Hollywood style song and dance)
('Dance with a Difference' song)

DOLORES: There. Now we're all family, arent't we?

HEDDY: I guess we do have certain bonds between us.

MAGDA: Do we? How? Besides the obvious one.

(An intimacy becomes apparent between Magda and Heddy that grows throughout the evening)

HEDDY: I suppose, the bond of people who have no bonds.

MAGDA: The loners of the Earth.

HEDDY: In our different ways.

MAGDA: Then aren't those kinds of bonds slender? Easily broken?

HEDDY: I wouldn't rely on them. They bind us to nothing but each other.

KAY: *(Bursting out)* A private detective doesn't belong to anybody but herself.

HEDDY: What has she got at the end of the day? Her Colt. 45 and a hip-flask of sasparilla?

KAY: Noboby wants to know you. Nobody. Not the Police, not the criminals, not even the clients. Least of all the clients. You do their shit work, to them you're shit.

DOLORES: Shame. I say that's a shame.

MAGDA: And our lone woman reporter, who'll never be one of the boys?

HEDDY: And always that little bit out of line with her editorial board. And our singer of songs? Our dream seller?

MAGDA: Dreams? They're on the house. It's something more tangible I need.

HEDDY: Then go for it.

MAGDA: *(Quietly)* I will.

DOLORES: *(Who has been drunkenly swaying on Kay's arm)* No husband no more *(Kisses Kay's cheek)*, no suburban house, no dogs, no dishwasher... *(Thinks)* It left a greasy mark on the glasses anyway, no...

KAY: I raise my glass... to the outsiders of this world.

MAGDA: Those without a stake in our great American democracy.

HEDDY: Oh, oh, careful now. That's dangerous.

MAGDA: Perhaps we are dangerous.

DOLORES: Even Victor's an outsider.

MAGDA: What makes you say that, Dolores?

DOLORES: I saw him taking packs of $100 bills out of the wall safe tonight. (Magda gets up) Any guy who owns a dive like this and has a suitcase full of greenbacks must be an outsider. Does that make sense? It seemed to at the time. (Magda starts towards the door) Magda, where are you going?

MAGDA: (Exiting) Get another bottle of bourbon. You'll have some more, won't you Kay?

KAY: (Calling after her) Magda, I'm teetotal. But, for you, tonight I had three glasses.

HEDDY: So? A fourth won't hurt.

KAY: What if a crime was committed here and now and I was drunk as a skunk?

HEDDY: I doubt if anyone would notice the difference.

KAY: You reckon? Hmm, maybe you're right. I guess I could handle it.

DOLORES: What we need is some music. Magda must sing for us.

HEDDY: She'll be tired. She's been singing all night.

DOLORES: But she'll sing for me, I know she will. (Magda reenters) Won't you, Magda?

MAGDA: What?

DOLORES: We want music.

MAGDA: Put on the jukebox.

DOLORES: No, you've got to sing Lana's theme.

MAGDA: I don't want to sing Lana's theme. Not tonight.

HEDDY: What do you want to sing, Magda?

MAGDA: (Thinks) A song my mother used to sing for me when I was a child. (She sings a Czechoslovak song. The mood becomes quieter)

(Dolores is sitting hunched in a corner. Kay is asleep. Heddy and Magda sit close together)

HEDDY: When did you come here?

MAGDA: When I was seven. Just before the Nazis invaded.

HEDDY: You never told me.

MAGDA: Told you what? That they would have deported me from the States, if I'd been a hostile witness? What did it matter to you?

HEDDY: A lot. You want to know something funny? Something real funny. I'm going to be in the same position as you.

MAGDA: The Committee?

HEDDY: An article I wrote for the Chronicle. Wanna see? (Brings it out)

MAGDA: (Reads) "The accusation of extreme left activism is a convenient weapon with which to smear trade union leadership and weaken the effectiveness of organised labour."

MAGDA: (Looking up) Your editor seen this?

HEDDY: No one has yet.

(Magda reads to herself as Heddy watches her, a look of yearning on her face. Magda looks up suddenly and Heddy looks away. After a pause Magda resumes reading aloud)

MAGDA: "Those still lucky enough to have a job are calling for halts to taxation, government spending, and more barriers against immigration. And so we have the perfect climate for the present Right-wing backlash and lack of effective opposition."
HEDDY: Well?
MAGDA: What can I say? You've decided to play heroine.
HEDDY: Someone's got to.
MAGDA: One solo voice? Forget it. There won't be no choir joining in.
HEDDY: Yeah. Well, I'm sick of keeping my mouth shut like a good girl.
MAGDA: *(Musingly)* You know, Dolores has this idea that you can be living in two different times zones at once. With her, of course, it's in a movie with Lana Hope. *(Abruptly)* You want me to be honest, Heddy? *(Picks up article)* I'm jealous as hell of this. Don't you think I'd give anything to have another chance? Another chance to be brave, make the right choices. *(Pause)* *(Quietly)* And don't you know that, given another chance, I'd make the same decisions all over again.
HEDDY: Don't talk defeated, Magda. It doesn't suit you. And things can change.
MAGDA: No, I guess I've landed with what I deserve.
HEDDY: Don't you want more? You can't settle for less than the best. Not you. Anyone but you, Magda.
MAGDA: You're sounding like Dolores. *(Reaches out and touches her)* Where's my cynical reporter gone?

(Dolores rises and goes out of the room)

HEDDY: Magda, there's something I have to tell you.
MAGDA: No, not now. *(Pause)* Yes, I do want more, O I think about it sometimes—Going back out West. Being... a star again. I will one day, you know. I'll fight my way back, one of these days.
HEDDY: Suppose they had a part right now that only you could do?
MAGDA: I'd be on the next plane.

(Dolores re-enters)

MAGDA: How you doing, honey?
DOLORES: Victor.
HEDDY: What about him?

DOLORES: He's sitting in the chair behind his desk, underneath Lana. There's a hole right in the middle of his forehead and the blood's dripping into the hair on the backs of his hands. *(She starts to laugh)* He looks disgusting. Why did it have to be underneath Lana?

(Her laughing turns to sobs. Magda puts her arm round her. Heddy goes out)

KAY: *(Waking up)* What's going on? Gee, I must have dropped off. Did I miss anything?

MAGDA: Just a murder, it seems.

HEDDY: *(Returns, shaking head)* One that came and went just as quick. There's nothing there.

DOLORES: I saw it, I tell you. The body.

HEDDY: Dolores, there's no body. The office is empty. Go see for yourself.

DOLORES: I saw it. I saw it. It was there.

MAGDA: Come on to bed, honey. *(Pulls her up and starts to lead her away. She stops in front of Heddy)* Goodnight, Heddy. Thanks.

HEDDY: For what?

MAGDA: For what you said.

HEDDY: And what I didn't say?

MAGDA: That too. Goodnight, Kay. *(She leaves with Dolores)*

KAY: Will somebody tell me how I missed a murder? How can some guy get himself killed and then unkilled in a matter of minutes?

HEDDY: That problem should keep you going till you hit the sack. Come on, Kay.

(Black-out)

ACT ONE
SCENE SIXTEEN

(London. Ella's flat later that same evening)
(There is a knock at the door. Ella appears in her dressing gown)

MONIKA: O, Miss Ford, I am sorry. I just came to borrow some coffee, but if I'd known you'd already gone to bed... it's just that I heard you and your friend...

ELLA: It must have been the radio. I'll turn it down.

MONIKA: No, don't worry about that. It's just these walls, they're so thin you can't help but hear everyone else's business.

ELLA: *(Coldly)* I think it's the duty of a neighbour *not* to listen to other people's affairs.

MONIKA: Back home in Germany before the war they said it was the duty of a neighbour, of a good citizen even, to listen for everything...

ELLA: Well, you're in England now.

MONIKA: ... and then to report it to the authorities. Now that's bad. Me, I'm just a nosey old woman, I just listen. Well, it harms no one.

ELLA: But it can make people very cross.

MONIKA: I take an interest in what's going on. My husband would say— 'Monika, you know what curiosity did for the cat?' He didn't take an interest in anything.

ELLA: Perhaps you should pay more attention to your husband, Mrs. Benz.

MONIKA: That would be difficult—he died last month.

ELLA: Oh. I didn't realise.

MONIKA: Because you don't take an interest.

ELLA: I'm sorry.

MONIKA: What's the difference? He'd been dead for years.

ELLA: Now you must excuse me. *(Trying to get her out)*

MONIKA: Excuse you for what, Miss Ford? What have you done? You know on the news tonight I heard a terrible thing. They say there are so many unemployed now the Government can't afford to give them rent. Isn't that bad?

ELLA: Very unfortunate.

MONIKA: My Estelle is unemployed, but she's got a home. A lot of young people aren't so lucky. They won't have anywhere. Then what? That's what I ask myself. Then what? Goodnight, Miss Ford.

(As she goes, Dagmar emerges in a dressing gown)

ELLA: That woman's insufferable.

DAGMAR: And so the spies are spied upon.

ELLA: *(Pacing)* We must keep our voices down in future.

DAGMAR: What did you take her parting remarks to mean?

ELLA: Her what? O nothing. She'll gabble on about anything till you actually throw her out.

DAGMAR: But to mention something so pertinent to the Department.

ELLA: She couldn't have seen you come in. You can't see the back entrance from her window. In future we must be more discreet.

DAGMAR: *(With the hint of a threat)* Or if Special Branch knew...

ELLA: *(Sharply)* What?

DAGMAR: *(Laughing)* They'd tell you—you better *come* quietly.

(Black-out)

ACT ONE
SCENE SEVENTEEN

(In the bar early afternoon the next day)

KAY: I been staking out Cordoni's territory this morning. Everyone's jittery on the streets.

HEDDY: Makes sense when you think Cordoni packed a pound of lead just a few days back.

KAY: No, things should have cooled by now. But right across the board, they're all scared out of their pants. The dealers, the pimps, the collection boys—even the doorman at Luigi's.

HEDDY: So what's going on?

KAY: I don't know. Nor do they. That's why they're nervous. How does Victor seem?

HEDDY: I haven't seen him around today.

MAGDA: *(Entering)* Victor's flown to Miami. Didn't I tell you?

KAY: Taking a vacation?

MAGDA: He's found himself a little diversion—name of Lola. I'll be running things here till he gets back.

KAY: Hmm, nice timing.

MAGDA: What do you mean?

KAY: Things seem to be getting a little hot round town, and Victor takes a vacation.

HEDDY: Makes sense. He'd be the first to save his skin.

DOLORES: *(Entering, looking very pale and drawn)* Nobody believes me.

MAGDA: Dolores, I told you to stay in bed. Come on, get some rest.

DOLORES: You all think I'm lying, don't you? Well, don't you?

MAGDA: We just think we were all a little drunk last night.

DOLORES: So I imagined it all? That's what you're saying to each other. That's what you're thinking, isn't it? That I'm crazy?

KAY: Well, there was nothing there when Heddy went to look.

DOLORES: So she says. Did anyone check to see if she was lying? Maybe she got rid of the body while she was out there. Maybe she did it. *(Kay leaves the room quietly)*

HEDDY: O, come on, Dolores.

DOLORES: Ask her about the $5000 she owed Victor. Go on, ask her.

HEDDY: How the hell did you know about that?

DOLORES: The jerk kept all his important papers in a heap on his desk. He was a fool as well as a horny bastard. Why he even had a press-cutting from yesterday's paper ringed round in ink...

MAGDA: Dolores, this is getting us nowhere. Victor's in Florida. He told me yesterday he was going.

DOLORES: He's been murdered, I tell you.

HEDDY: For God's sake be logical. How can you have a murder without a body?

KAY: *(Re-entering)* Victor the type who eats hamburgers?

MAGDA: What?

KAY: Onion, pickle, relish, lots of tomato sauce?

DOLORES: Victor hated hamburgers.

MAGDA: Why?

KAY: There's a red stain on the carpet under his desk.

HEDDY: You think it's blood?

KAY: Could be.

HEDDY: This whole thing is ridiculous. If Victor had a hole in his head like Dolores says, he could hardly have got up, walked out and took a flight to Miami.

DOLORES: He didn't. Someone got rid of the body. That someone could only have been you.

HEDDY: There was no body.

KAY: But, if there was one, and Dolores did see it...

HEDDY: But I didn't.

KAY: ... and someone got rid of it before Heddy went into the office... who did the murder?

DOLORES: *(Pointing to Heddy)* Her.

KAY: Someone could have come into the office while we were out here having the party. They could have shot Victor, heard Dolores coming and hid, then removed the body before Heddy got there.

MAGDA: Quite a busy little murderer.

KAY: Or... there is another explanation.

HEDDY: What's that?

KAY: It was one of us. Everyone here left the room at some time last night.

DOLORES: But only she could have got rid of the body, so that proves it.

MAGDA: Or maybe one of us went in and killed him, then rang the city waste disposal and had them collect. For Christ's sake, I'm tired of this game. I'm beginning to feel like I'm in some kind of B movie. Victor is in Florida. I'm expecting him to telegraph. When he does, maybe you'll all cool it. Now, if you want to play detectives, go do it some place else. I'm tired and I've got the accounts to finish.

(Black-out)

ACT ONE
SCENE EIGHTEEN

(In the bar, later that day)

MAGDA: Dolores, I want to talk to you. We won't say anything more about what you didn't see last night. When you're in the wrong it's hard to back down afterwards. Maybe you even begin to believe it yourself. That's how it is, isn't it, Dolores?

DOLORES: Yes, Magda, I guess that's how it is.

MAGDA: I know why you started this whole number. It was because of something you thought you saw, wasn't it? Something that made you jealous. And scared.

DOLORES: She never took her eyes off you all last night. Don't you see what she's trying to do? She's trying to come between us.

MAGDA: Now how could she do that? Tell me, huh?

DOLORES: *(Suddenly relaxing)* She can't. I'm being silly, aren't I, Magda?

MAGDA: Very silly.

DOLORES: Nobody can come between us.

MAGDA: That's right. Rub my shoulders a little, Honey.

DOLORES: She's stupid to think she can. Just there?

MAGDA: Mm, that's wonderful.

DOLORES: Poor darling. Is it Dolores that's made you so tense? I guess I just have too much imagination sometimes.

MAGDA: Just a little maybe.

DOLORES: But it's better, isn't it, than having none. Like her. *(Imitates Heddy)* Be logical, Dolores. You've got to look at the facts, Dolores. Facts are facts are facts…

MAGDA: *(Laughing)* You're a cruel mimic.

DOLORES: Life's more than her dry old facts. When she talks she strips the flesh and blood off a thing.

MAGDA: It's her way of being honest. To go on peeling away till she gets to the bare bones.

DOLORES: So who wants to cosy up to a skeleton? Is that living?

MAGDA: She's a journalist. And a good one. She tries to write the truth.

DOLORES: I don't understand that way of looking at things. I'm not clever like her. But what I feel is as real as what she writes down on paper, isn't it? You know what I think? I think that with all her facts and bare bones, she only ever gets at half the truth. She misses out the part that really matters.

MAGDA: And what's that, Dolores? What really matters?

DOLORES: I don't think I can explain properly. I don't know as I can describe it.

MAGDA: Maybe because it's indescribable. It comes in shreds, in whispers, in half-light.

(During the following 5 lines the last syllable(s) of each speech overlap(s) with the first syllable(s) of the next, as indicated by a slash)

DOLORES: When I'm asleep, I dream sometimes I'm running down a path in a high forest, and it's just ahead/of me.

MAGDA: Always/just out of/reach.

DOLORES: I try/to catch it, hold it, just for a/moment.

MAGDA: And/it disappears between your/fingers.

DOLORES: Whenever/there was something I couldn't keep hold of, couldn't put a name to, I'd call it/Lana.

MAGDA: Lana./

("Time" song)

ACT ONE
SCENE NINETEEN

(Later that day)
(Magda enters the office and sees Kay crawling around)

MAGDA: Still looking for bloodstains?

KAY: *(Starts guiltily and puts something behind her back)* Well, you know how it is—the life of a private detective can be very dull. Divorce cases, alimony, missing Chihuahuas—it's kind of a break to get a real mystery.

MAGDA: Even a manufactured one? I got the telegram from Victor here. Arrived just now. Want to verify? *(Shows her telegram from Miami)*.

KAY: Miami, huh.

MAGDA: *(A little patronisingly)* Florida. Where Victor said he was going, remember? Mystery cleared up?

KAY: Well, I guess that's that then.

MAGDA: I guess so.

KAY: I guess if a telegram says it comes from a place, then it comes from that place where it says it comes from.

MAGDA: That would seem the general idea, yes. Unless Wells Fargo are part of a big conspiracy.

(Kay rubs her nose vigorously and sneezes. Magda stares at her)

KAY: Must be a high pollen count round here. Oh well, *(She starts to sidle out still hiding something behind her back)* I guess it's back to the Chihuahuas. Here, pooch, pooch...

MAGDA: Kay, what have you got behind your back?

KAY: Behind my back? Behind my... Oh, you mean, behind my back?

MAGDA: *(Dryly)* I believe that is what I said.

(Kay produces a magazine, but it is apparent to the audience, though not to Magda, that she is still hiding something else)

KAY: O, it's a copy of Silver Screen. Yeah, that's what it is. This week's. I found it in the trash can.

MAGDA: How did it get there?

KAY: I guess Dolores must have finished with it.

MAGDA: She never throws them. She has a stack a mile high, going back ten years. Must have got in there by mistake. I'll take it. *(Laughs)* No need to look so guilty.

KAY: Huh?

MAGDA: About reading it. Why, I might even take a look at this myself.

ACT ONE
SCENE TWENTY

(In the bar, immediately after)

KAY: Ah, Heddy, just the person I was looking for. I've been doing a spot of investigation…

HEDDY: Kay, would you say I'm a normal, relatively sane individual?

KAY: Normal? Hm, that depends on how you look at things. *I* think so. Some people would say different. As for sanity, again there's no Richter scale…

HEDDY: O.K., O.K., I wasn't asking for a lesson in philosophy.

KAY: But I guess you've got your head screwed on more than most.

HEDDY: So why do I feel like a wired up, over-the-top adolescent?

KAY: You want me to hazard a guess?

HEDDY: Is it that obvious?

KAY: My nose told me the first day. If ever there was a dame that spelt trouble, it's her.

HEDDY: So I've got to pull myself together, right?

KAY: Right.

HEDDY: Take a long, cool look at things, right?

KAY: Right.

HEDDY: Keep a sense of proportion, right?

KAY: Right.

HEDDY: Go to hell.

KAY: Right. *(Turns to go)* O, before I go, I wanted to ask you something. Victor, is he political?

HEDDY: No more than most American citizens. He gripes at his tax returns, thinks socialised medicine is a communist plot, and that God loves America. Pretty much Joe Average.

KAY: I found the paragraph Dolores said he'd ringed round. It was in the trash can, torn into little pieces. I managed to gum most of it together.

(Kay holds out a bit of paper that's stuck to her fingers)

HEDDY: And yourself to it, I see. What's it say?

KAY: It's the piece about Pedroza holing out in New York. Now why should Victor be interested in that?

HEDDY: And interested enough to cut it out and ring it round. Good question.

KAY: If it had been the bit about Cordoni that would have made sense.

HEDDY: Why should Victor give a damn about a South American revolutionary?

KAY: That's where you got me stuck.

(Puts hand on Heddy's arm. Because of the glue she's been using, it attaches itself and moves where Kay's does, till Heddy pulls away in irritation)

INTERVAL

ACT TWO
SCENE ONE

(London. Ella's flat shortly after the end of the last London scene)

DAGMAR: I'm just sick to death of living a lie.

ELLA: You have a choice. Throw it all up, job, career, prospects. Chop off your hair and wear a badge if you want to label yourself like a piece of left luggage. But don't expect me to be anywhere in sight when you make your empty gestures...

DAGMAR: Empty gestures? Is that what you call being true to yourself?

ELLA: Being true... I never suspected you could be so melodramatic. Do you seriously expect me to believe all this extreme lefty nonsense?

DAGMAR: Don't you think I'm capable of making the sacrifice?

ELLA: You? No. You fought your way up to the class you felt you belonged to, and to the position and lifestyle you've got now. You're more of a social snob than I am. You know where your loyalties, and your interests lie.

DAGMAR: Because you have no convictions of your own, you can't understand people who do.

ELLA: To be unemployed now! Unemployable if you pull a stunt like that. No, not with your inside knowledge, Dagmar. Voluntarily become a 'recipient' of "Operation Guesthouse"?

DAGMAR: *(Suddenly quiet)* That remark was an extremely careless one for you.

ELLA: *(Unnerved)* A slip of the tongue.

DAGMAR: A dangerous one in the wrong company. Like an 'extreme lefty'.

(Ella stares hard at her)

ELLA: *(In a low voice)* Pack up your things and get out.
DAGMAR: What? Look, Ella, I was only joking.
ELLA: I no longer trust you, and I take no risks.
DAGMAR: I'm sorry. I was being silly...
ELLA: You've had your chance.
DAGMAR: Just one? Is that all I get?
ELLA: That's all anyone ever gets.
DAGMAR: Jesus, you're ruthless. Not just to me, to yourself. Where are *your* loyalties when it comes to your own feelings?
ELLA: They don't enter into it.
DAGMAR: So that's it? We're finished, just like that?
ELLA: I thought I'd made that clear. As far as I am concerned you no longer exist.
DAGMAR: Ella, don't banish me like this, please.
ELLA: Go.
DAGMAR: Your life is tyrannised by secrecy. A true undercover! The real Ella never sees the light of day. Creeping about like a thief in the night, taking your forbidden pleasures where you can. I can't live like that.
ELLA: That has become obvious. But it's a sentiment that will be your downfall.
DAGMAR: Perhaps. But on the way down, Ella, I'm going to take you with me.

(Dagmar exits, and leaves a petrified Ella. Ella at length picks up the phone)

ELLA: Section 303. C for Cobra? This is Z for Zebra. There's a matter that needs to be attended to. Yes, E for Exit. Urgently.

(Black-out)
("Odd girl out" song)

ACT TWO
SCENE TWO

(New York. In the bar a few days after the last New York scene)

HEDDY: Dolores suspects.
MAGDA: I know.
HEDDY: I guess it's wrong. I feel bad, but I can't help it.
MAGDA: There's nothing to feel bad about.

HEDDY: Not yet, no. But things can hardly stay like they are. *(Magda doesn't answer)* Magda, I've been thinking. This article—once I hand it over, we both know what that means. It won't be easy for me to get work here. And even if I did, what kind of hypocrisy is it for me to attack a system and go on accepting a meal ticket from it. If I really believe in what I say, I should leave America, go live in the Eastern bloc.

MAGDA: Always such scrupulous principles.

HEDDY: How else could I live with myself?

MAGDA: Other people manage. I do.

HEDDY: You're not happy.

MAGDA: Aren't I? Maybe I don't need to ask so much of myself. It's not required, you know.

HEDDY: I couldn't face the world if I didn't.

MAGDA: What the hell does the world care? My little Heddy, heroic gestures are only important to the people who make them.

HEDDY: Magda, I thought I might go to Czechoslavakia. And you could come with me. You could go home.

MAGDA: What? You must be crazy. America's my home. You think I want to go back there? You're out of your mind.

HEDDY: But when you sang your mother's song, you had tears…

MAGDA: That's called nostalgia, Baby. Hollywood's full of it. So you cry for that little girl way back running round in bare feet, doesn't mean you want to quit wearing shoes. I want glamour. I want stardom. I want money. I want to live.

HEDDY: But not at any price. I don't believe you really mean that, Magda.

MAGDA: You just don't want to believe it.

HEDDY: But that's not the whole story. There's a part of you that's better than that. Finer.

MAGDA: Jesus, what is it about me? For Dolores I'm Lana. For you I'm some revolutionary heroine. I can't fulfill those kind of fantasies. I'm me, Magda Thornton. Remember?

HEDDY: Sometimes another person can know you better than you know yourself. I see you clearly. I know the real Magda Thornton.

MAGDA: *(Starting to move away)* Well, maybe you'll introduce me sometime.

HEDDY: *(Pulling her back)* Magda, where does that leave me? Leave us?

MAGDA: Us? I never said there was an 'us'.

HEDDY: The other night your eyes said it.

MAGDA: *(Laughing)* I've been told I have wicked eyes. Is that another part of the 'real' me?

HEDDY: Magda, don't play with me.

MAGDA: So you want me to cheat on Dolores?

HEDDY: I'll never believe you really love her.

MAGDA: You don't think much of Dolores, do you?

HEDDY: I didn't say that. She's just not right for you.

MAGDA: But you see, I do care about her. She's very special person. And, you want me to be honest, she's very good in bed. *(Laughs)* Hey, come here. Whatever happens, Heddy, and I don't know what will, I'm not ready to give up Dolores. I'm certainly not going to Czechoslovakia. If I went anywhere, I'd go back West, to Hollywood.

HEDDY: I suppose Dolores didn't tell you about the movie, did she?

MAGDA: Which movie?

HEDDY: *(After a pause)* Nothing. Forget I said it.

(Black-out)

ACT TWO
SCENE THREE

(In Victor's office, the next day)

KAY: *(Alone)* O.K., so what have we got? Victor disappears, last seen with half a million bucks. Dolores saw him dead, Heddy didn't. It would seem Heddy is correct, because Magda has a telegram from him. *(Rubs nose violently)* Wait a minute, something wrong here. The date. I didn't see the date. Hmm. What else? Torn-up press cutting about a South American revolutionary. Half the New York underworld strung out. What does it all add up to? *(Rubbing ears now)* Goddam it, this itch is getting so bad, even my ears are blocking up. *(Phone rings. She picks it up)* Hello, excuse me a moment. *(Tries to clear sinuses as the phone voice speaks)*

VOICE: This is a warning…

KAY: A what? Just hold on, will you. *(Clears sinuses again)*

VOICE: Pedroza is a job for the big boys. Cordoni thought he was big enough, now he's on a slab in the morgue…

KAY: *(After final blow of nose)* That's better. What were you saying?

VOICE: Stay out of this or you'll find yourself in a little accident. A fatal one. *(The phone goes and with a click)*

KAY: Hey, wait a minute. Do you know you can be prosecuted for making threatening telephone calls? It's against the law. It's… hell, he's hung up on me, goddam it. Someone wanting to kill me. That's ridiculous. Well… no. I guess there's a lot of hoods out there who'd feel a whole lot safer if I was six feet under.

MAGDA: *(Voice off)* Dolores. *(Calling)* Dolores, I can't find my green dress. You're not wearing it again, are you?

KAY: Idiot! Idiot! The phone call wasn't for me. It was for Magda. They mistook me for her. Must have been my manner. Air of cool authority.

Nose, you have misled me. Magda isn't trouble. She's in trouble. O.K., I can handle this. Accident, huh? That could mean anything, any time.

MAGDA: *(At door)* Dolores... O, Kay, it's you.

KAY: Magda, I have to tell you I have reason to believe you're in deadly danger. And it'll be set up to look like an accident. But don't worry, I'm going to protect you.

(Kay takes Magda's arm and they both freeze as the lights fade. In the darkness headlights appear, the squeal of tyres, a scream, Kay pulls Magda out the way)

ACT TWO
SCENE FOUR

(London. A dark street)

KAY: Jeez, that was nearly curtains for both of us.

DAGMAR: Maniac driver. Came straight at us.

KAY: You O.K.?

DAGMAR: Just a few cuts, thanks to you. You saved my life.

KAY: Didn't I tell you I'd protect you, Madga?

DAGMAR: Magda? I'm afraid you've mistaken me for somebody else.

KAY: Huh? O God, you're in shock. Look, eh... stick your head between your knees or something, while I get a cab, take you home. Let's see, where are we? Doesn't look familiar. Which way would Ninth Street be from here, Magda?

DAGMAR: I'm not Magda and I live in Holland Park, and I'm perfectly alright now. Thank you. Goodnight. *(She is gone)*

KAY: *(Calling after her)* Magda, wait a minute. Hey, you dropped something... her wallet. *(Opens it)* Say, nice picture. Cute dress. Drivers licence. British?!! Dagmar Eergusson?! Dagmar... Born 23rd May 1958! What the... O, it's a misprint. I even nearly went to check with that billboard. *(Laughs at herself as she looks at it)* 'Lecture on Einstein's Theory of Time-Space Continuum'. Huh, sounds like a hit. Conway Hall... London! August 1st, 1985! Oh, oh, Kay, keep calm. It's O.K. Don't let it bother you. Just take a breath and say to yourself... "Help!" It's the rye. Why didn't I stick to sasparilla? Let me take this in. I'm in England. I've skipped three decades... Amnesia... For thirty years? I guess it happens. I must be 61. I don't feel 61. How would I know? I've never been 61 till now. Let me take a look in the wallet. Cashcard? Barclaycard? Access card? American Express card? Eurocheque card? This dame must be forever losing her door key. A couple of bills—sterling, and a few measly coins. She must be as poor as hell. That's tough. I got to get this back to her. Here's an address. Ella Ford, Flat 5, 203 St. Johns Wood Court. A friend, I guess.

(Looks up and around) St. Johns Wood Avenue. I must be just around the corner.

(Black-out)

ACT TWO
SCENE FIVE

(Ella's flat some minutes later)

KAY: *(Showing her photo in wallet)* Know this woman?

ELLA: I... eh... we work together.

KAY: Friend of yours?

ELLA: No, not really a friend. She's a younger woman, unsure of herself. I've tried to... show her the ropes.

KAY: *(Attempting humour)* Enough to hang herself, huh?

ELLA: What?

KAY: Little joke.

ELLA: Look, who are you?

KAY: Detective.

ELLA: C.I.D.?

KAY: Huh? Oh, you want to see my I.D. *(Fishes in pocket)* It's a special...

ELLA: Special Branch. I see. I didn't think they'd involve you lot. Well, what's the problem?

KAY: Your friend was in a little car accident...

ELLA: *(Recoiling)* Oh. But I thought she'd just be picked up.

KAY: Picked up? O, no time.

ELLA: Well, I realise the urgency, of course. But that...

KAY: Just a quick push, that was all.

ELLA: That wasn't necessary.

KAY: O, it was.

ELLA: *(Taking hold of herself)* Yes, yes, of course. There's too much at stake.

KAY: Anyway, to put your mind at rest, she's absolutely fine. Because I was there.

ELLA: You were there? Just you?

KAY: Yup. Lucky for her.

ELLA: Did she talk?

KAY: Talk? O yeah. She talked fine.

ELLA: *(Carefully)* How much does your Department know of this?

KAY: My Depart... O, no. lady. I'm working solo.

ELLA: *(In relief)* I see. That's different. Perks on the side. Extra pocket money for a bit of graft. I understand.

KAY: *(To herself)* I wish I did.

ELLA: I think we can come to some arrangement. I'll say that I'm very concerned about the welfare of this unfortunate girl. She's obviously highly unstable, mentally, and a danger to herself. I'd like to help her.

KAY: Well now, that's mighty kind of you.

ELLA: Don't try to be funny. That's the story, alright? I want you to find her and bring her here.

KAY: But I've got no idea where she is.

ELLA: Try the Artemis Club, 132 Upper Grosvenor.

KAY: Club, huh?

ELLA: Yes, a ladies' club. You know, like Gentlemen's clubs.

KAY: Only for ladies?

ELLA: That's right. Perfectly above board. Well, go on. What are you waiting for?

KAY: You mean, right now?

ELLA: This minute. There's no time to lose.

KAY: I'm pretty bushed. I was hoping to be able to find a bed and shack down...

ELLA: *(Staring at her)* My God, the world is full of us. *(Trying to sound seductive, caressing her)* Perhaps we can arrange that afterwards. I'll look forward to it.

KAY: Uh? Oh... yeah, sure thing... but actually, what I had in mind right now was... what do you call it? ... a guesthouse.

ELLA: Fool.

KAY: Was that the wrong word? Well, there's no need to be impolite.

ELLA: *(To herself)* So Dagmar's already started blabbing her mouth off...

KAY: *(Scratching her nose)* Oops, danger.

ELLA: Yes, an emergency. We can only avert it if you hurry.

KAY: This dame must be in a bad way.

ELLA: To the Artemis!

KAY: Right.

ELLA: Get a cab. But not outside this door.

KAY: Right. Oh, eh... a little problem...

ELLA: What is it now?

KAY: Money.

ELLA: Of course, we've all got our price. You'll be well paid, don't worry. Wait, here's a first instalment. *(Hands her notes)* Now go. Quick. *(Kay exits)* The fools. What were they playing at? Handling the thing like some fifties 'B' movie. And then bungling the job. Amateurs. Now, when Dagmar gets here... when she gets here... God, I must keep myself together. *(Suddenly breaks)* O Dagmar, why did it have to be like this? Forgive me. Because I know very well what I'm going to do.

(Black-out)

ACT TWO
SCENE SIX

(New York. In the bar. Afternoon. Heddy and Magda embrace as Kay watches furtively)

HEDDY: You look so beautiful.

MAGDA: How do you know? You're looking over my shoulder.

HEDDY: I can see you in the mirror. I can see those delicious soft hairs on the nape of your neck. I can see the curve of your shoulder muscle. I can see... Kay!! What the hell! What are you?—some kind of voyeur?... or... my God, has Dolores hired you to spy on us? *(Grabs Kay)*

KAY: *(In a stranglehold)* What you are doing is technically known as attempted assault in the Criminal Code...

HEDDY: It'll become attempted murder, unless you give me an answer fast.

KAY: *(With dignity)* I do not snoop on my friends. And I wouldn't get myself mixed up with what you're doing—it's too messy.

HEDDY: So what the hell *are* you up to?

KAY: I'm merely trying to protect Magda.

HEDDY: Who from?

KAY: Eh... I don't know.

MAGDA: Kay is convinced that someone is trying to kill me. So she sticks closer to me than a pickpocket after a wallet.

KAY: *(To herself)* Wallet? Now why should that ring bells?

MAGDA: I'm surprised you didn't try to get in bed with us. But frankly, Kay, I'm sick of all this. I want you out from under my feet. Understand?

KAY: Sure. O.K. Fine. Understood. I'll back off. O, by the way, I... eh... picked up this emerald pin down-town today. *(Kay gives it to her)* Thought it might match your eyes.

HEDDY: *(Still angry)* It won't.

MAGDA: But I think it will. How kind of you, Kay. And how unexpected.

HEDDY: I don't like it. It bugs me.

KAY: O no, it's not you it'll bug... I mean, eh... Make sure you wear it now.

MAGDA: I shall pin it on my bosom... Right here. O.K.?

KAY: Eh, should be.

MAGDA: *(Seductively)* And I shall think of you as I wear it. As though we were in touch. *(Touches her)*

KAY: *(Blushing)* O, eh, yeah, we will be. *(Exits rather flustered. Magda laughs)*

HEDDY: Do you have to flirt with everyone?

MAGDA: Why not? It gave her pleasure.

HEDDY: You can't give pleasure to every woman you meet.

MAGDA: No? *(Laughs)* Come on, it was just a little diversion.

HEDDY: Don't I divert you enough?

MAGDA: I do believe you're jealous.

HEDDY: Of course I'm jealous. I don't know what's happening to me—I seem to spend my life waiting for those few hours when we're together.

MAGDA: And when we are? Isn't it worth it?

HEDDY: I guess expectations diminish. You learn to accept the little on offer.

MAGDA: Thanks a lot. I sound like something on a five and dime counter.

HEDDY: (Hastily) Yes, of course it's worth it. Magda, when will I see you again?

MAGDA: I'll be singing here tonight as usual.

HEDDY: You really enjoy it, don't you? You get a kick out of it?

MAGDA: Out of what?

HEDDY: Having such power over me.

MAGDA: Don't you? Doesn't my hard-headed woman of the world enjoy a little surrender? Isn't that part of the fantasy? For a short while you can drop all responsibility in exchange for a dream.

HEDDY: Is that what you think love is? My love.

MAGDA: Your love. Everyone's. For you I'm thirty years of need parcelled into a good body, a pretty face, and, most of all, female.

HEDDY: You have a low opinion of me.

MAGDA: You're no different from anyone else, although you like to think you are. I studied people a lot for my profession. That's what made me a great actress. Still makes me a great actress.

HEDDY: Has Dolores said anything yet?

MAGDA: About what? About you, you mean? No, she doesn't mention you. I guess she thinks you've admitted defeat.

HEDDY: God, how I hate doing this to her.

MAGDA: O cut the moral cliche, Heddy. It might help out your self-esteem, but it doesn't impress me none. I'd respect you more if you just came out and said, you don't give a damn about Dolores.

HEDDY: But I do. Magda, inside I'm a mess. I just can't help what I'm doing.

MAGDA: So whose fault is it? The weather? The government? The guy who runs the hamburger stall on the corner? Heddy, we go through this every time. Go find someone else to take confessional for you, and leave me out of it.

HEDDY: But you're right in it. We're both doing the dirty on Dolores.

MAGDA: That's right. But I'm not the one bellyaching about it.

HEDDY: Don't you feel ashamed too?

MAGDA: If I want something enough I won't stop till I have it. And enjoy.

HEDDY: And you want me enough?

MAGDA: I guess. But I won't beat myself up about it.

HEDDY: There's something totally ruthless about you. It scares me.

MAGDA: I always scare people when I'm being truthful. It's a good thing I don't do it too often.

HEDDY: You can shrug off betraying a friend…

MAGDA: You were all set to betray your country.

HEDDY: Does a lesbian have a country? Anyway, I still haven't decided what to do about the article. I might send it in yet... O, I don't know what the hell to do. I'd be fired. It would mean leaving New York. Leaving you. And for what?

MAGDA: Wasn't it to safeguard your integrity?

HEDDY: Maybe it's the best for all concerned if I just go away some place and lose myself.

MAGDA: *(Flippantly)* Try L.A. The weather's good, and you can lose yourself on the freeway, no problem.

HEDDY: Be serious, Madga.

MAGDA: How can I, a mere mortal, grapple with that mythical conscience of yours?

HEDDY: *(Piqued)* Maybe I will go away, for a while. Maybe I'm just too available.

MAGDA: So who's getting sulky?

HEDDY: I don't think you'd even notice.

MAGDA: Heddy. *(No response)* Heddy, I'm talking to you.

HEDDY: What?

MAGDA: Come over here.

HEDDY: Say you don't want me to go.

MAGDA: *(Smiling)* Would that help the struggle?

HEDDY: Say it.

MAGDA: I don't want you to go. *(Kisses her)* But you'll have to just for now, Dolores'll be back. Silver Screen, mm. Still haven't got round to reading it. *(Picks it up)*

HEDDY: *(Quietly)* Maybe you should, Magda, maybe you should.

MAGDA: Yeah, I'll do that. *(Exits)*

KAY: *(Entering)* Heddy...

HEDDY: Not now, Kay.

KAY: Look, it's O.K. You know I wouldn't betray you. *(Heddy stares)* I mean, we're still friends, right?

HEDDY: Kay, you got any silver on you?

KAY: *(Putting hand in pocket)* Sure. How much do you want?

HEDDY: Try thirty pieces.

KAY: Huh?

(Black-out)

ACT TWO
SCENE SEVEN

(London. Ella's flat, sound of knocking)

ELLA: Dagmar, Thank God, darli… *(Sees it's Monika)*
MONIKA: I just came to return the coffee I borrowed, Miss Ford.
ELLA: Coffee?… O, O, thank you. You really needn't have bothered… *(As Monika stares at her)* Such a nuisance, I seem to have got something in my eye.
MONIKA: Tears, perhaps. Such unhappiness, I think.
ELLA: Happiness. That's a luxury few of us can afford.
MONIKA: I am sorry for you.
ELLA: Please don't bother to be. I'm perfectly alright, I assure you.
MONIKA: Such admirable self-control you have, Miss Ford. The upper lip so stiff always.
ELLA: I despise people who "betray" their feelings.
MONIKA: And yet, you betray your feelings a lot. I think. Small, daily treacheries. They are necessary in your job.
ELLA: My job?
MONIKA: Yes, I think they must be.
ELLA: What do you know about my job?
MONIKA: You are a strange person, Miss Ford. At the centre of such a big, busy machine, that runs this society and controls all our lives—and yet, you don't belong. You are an outsider.
ELLA: I don't know what you're talking about.
MONIKA: Intelligence.
ELLA: What!
MONIKA: You have intelligence. You know what I'm talking about. You are always so clever, Miss Ford. Never do you give away anything. But you see, that is your mistake. Everyone round here, they are very concerned. The Government send in bulldozers to make a big wasteland. Then they fence it round with barbed wire. So everyone wants to know—"what is going on?" There are petitions, public meetings, conversations on street corners. Only *you* don't join in. In Germany, that's how we knew. When the first lorries came early one morning, nobody could believe this was happening. But the grocerman, he didn't look surprised at all.
ELLA: Perhaps he was simply a man who minded his own business.
MONIKA: In Germany at that time, too many people minded their own business. Now, when I hear you crying through the wall as though your heart would break…
ELLA: I will not be spied upon like this, do you hear? Can't I get any privacy? Will I never be left alone?
MONIKA: Is that what you really want? So proud you are, Miss Ford. So well hidden what's inside. The hands that reach out to you, you push away.
ELLA: Because I don't need them. I'm perfectly capable of looking after myself.

MONIKA: But if, one day, you slip, who will be there to catch you? Your friend, she has gone now?

ELLA: *(Seems about to lose her temper, then suddenly turns away miserably)* Yes, she's gone now.

MONIKA: In the camp, I had a friend. When they took Erika, I thought I, too, would die. The cold in winter was terrible, freezing the body. But worse was the loneliness—that freezes the soul.

ELLA: *(Dully)* Perhaps the soul is better left frozen.

MONIKA: What I most desired was denied me. What you hunger for, you deny yourself.

ELLA: One can't have everything. In this life one must make certain choices. And you, haven't you denied yourself? After all, you chose to marry.

MONIKA: Frederik? We understood each other. And he never asked for much. Never made demands.

ELLA: How lucky to find such an ideal solution.

MONIKA: Some people you can persecute, torture and humiliate, and afterwards they demand nothing. They accept to live is to suffer. Others, they demand a state, a nation, so they will never have to suffer again. And now there is a new wandering tribe of Canaan, without a home. But, for that, the world must take responsibility. If they had not persecuted for so long, had not made outsiders... and you, Miss Ford, such a beautiful home you have, but where do you belong?

ELLA: I belong to this society. I've taken great pains to ensure I am not an outcast.

MONIKA: Great pain, for sure.

ELLA: Yes, alright. But I am accepted. I have made myself acceptable. That's what counts. Even if it has... been through subterfuge...

MONIKA: Such a good training for your profession.

(Pause. They look at each other)

ELLA: I love my country.

MONIKA: Even when it is wrong. In 1939 Germany was wrong. Should I have loved it then?

ELLA: That's different.

MONIKA: You think so?

ELLA: Here the question of loyalty is very clear.

MONIKA: No, no. This is a deeply divided country. Like the heart. I think then it is not so clear as you want to believe, when you talk of loyalty. What you do is bad, you know. Very bad.

ELLA: Whether I agreed with you or not wouldn't make one iota of difference.

MONIKA: Every country and every person must learn one day. What you reject, what you repress, what you force down into the ground, these things do not disappear. Some day they will rise, and when they do, there will be no controlling them.

(Black-out)

ACT TWO
SCENE EIGHT

(London. Dagmar in the Artemis club, pretty drunk. Kay handing her her wallet)

DAGMAR: Well, the woman who saved my life. And now you've taken all this trouble to return my wallet. What a charmingly kind world it is, outside of my profession.

KAY: Well, to be quite honest, this wasn't the whole reason I came.

DAGMAR: *(Looking her up and down)* Let me buy you a drink. Perhaps you can help me again.

KAY: I'd be happy to.

DAGMAR: Help relieve this burden here... *(Puts hand on breast)*

KAY: Eh... um...

DAGMAR: Of self-despising and nausea. *(Gulps back drink)*

KAY: Oh, if you feel nauseous, I'd advise sasparilla...

DAGMAR: Saspar... *(Laughs)* You know, I think you're going to prove rather diverting.

KAY: Thank you. Say, this is some place here. Real fancy.

DAGMAR: *(Suddenly tense)* You have been in a 'ladies' club before, haven't you?

KAY: O sure.

DAGMAR: Good. You looked as though you had.

KAY: I been in plenty of dives, but nothing classy like this.

DAGMAR: Money can at least buy an exclusive setting for 'perversion', if nothing else. *(Strokes Kay's hair)* You know, you're rather nice.

KAY: *(To herself)* Geez, this is the second time in an hour. I think I'm going to enjoy being 61. I guess everyone likes an older woman.

DAGMAR: *(Still stroking her hair)* I'm being very forward and I don't even know your name. *(Puts her arm round Kay)*

KAY: Just call me Kay.

DAGMAR: *(Recoiling)* K? K for...?

KAY: Just plain Kay.

DAGMAR: *(Hurriedly whipping arm away)* Of course... how silly of me... in your section even code names are classified.

KAY: What happened to the arm?

DAGMAR: *(Backing off even more)* O, one must keep up appearances in these kind of places, you understand? In order to pass. Naturally, I find it all very distasteful myself.

KAY: Yeah, it's tough. But you've just got to pretend sometimes.

DAGMAR: Yes, even though it's quite against my nature.

KAY: Yeah, I can see that. I can tell when someone's straightforward.

(A pause in which Dagmar looks relieved but jittery and Kay is wondering how to continue) Now, eh... Ella Ford...

DAGMAR: O, God! Of course! That's why you're here. My progress with her was... monitored.

KAY: *(At a loss)* Eh... pretty much.

DAGMAR: I can assure you she didn't have a clue.

KAY: *(Aside)* She's not the only one.

DAGMAR: I played my part very well.

KAY: *(Aside)* Hm, she said this dame was a little cookie in the head. Maybe thinks she's an actress. Better humour her. *(Aloud)* Stunning performance. Shame Sam Goldwyn didn't catch it on celluloid.

DAGMAR: Well it wouldn't have received an X rating. Just enough to make me... plausible.

KAY: And you were. Very convincing. Like a natural.

DAGMAR: Which I'm not!

KAY: Must have done a lot of practising then. *(Dagmar is terrified)* Eh, now why don't you go see Ella Ford...

DAGMAR: But I understood my role was over.

KAY: O yeah, well you played it so well, we feel you should go right ahead and do some more for us.

DAGMAR: Well, of course, if it's an order...

KAY: Straight from the director.

DAGMAR: Really? Well, in that case... will that mean promotion?

KAY: You'll be a star. Like Lana.

DAGMAR: Lana?

KAY: Did you say Lana?

DAGMAR: No, you said it.

KAY: I did? Now why should I say that? *(Begins to hum Lana's theme)*

DAGMAR: *(Her face suddenly in pain)* I can't do it.

KAY: *(Distractedly)* Sure you can.

DAGMAR: I've done my part. Can't someone else take over now? I can't face her again. Not after the way I've acted.

KAY: *(Still humming. Still distracted)* You acted swell. That's why you got to be there for the curtains.

DAGMAR: *(In anguish)* O, Ella, forgive me. Maybe if I had the choice all over again...

(Suddenly Kay stops humming. Dagmar resumes her former self)

KAY: O.K. Ready?
DAGMAR: *(Businesslike)* Yes. You'll be recording it all, I suppose?
KAY: *(Still humouring)* Sure will. Every word.
DAGMAR: And your role? I presume one of my new comrades, on the extreme left?
KAY: Sure, sure, Right off-stage, if that's what you want.

(Black-out)

ACT TWO
SCENE NINE

(New York. Kay is in one spotlight fiddling with a tape recorder, earphones on, twiddling knobs. In another spot Magda is flicking through silver screen and rustling the material of her dress. Suddenly these sounds come through Kay's headphones very loud, blasting her out. She takes them off and rubs her ears. The phone rings. Magda moves towards it as Dolores enters and picks it up. Spot fades on Kay. She freezes)

DOLORES: *(In Magda's voice)* Hello, yes? This is Magda speaking…
VOICE: About the contract…
MAGDA: *(Tearing receiver from Dolores)* What the hell are you doing? Give me that phone. Hello?
VOICE: We've located him. Everything's set.
MAGDA: Good. Get it done fast. Before anyone else gets there first.
VOICE: O.K. The contract's out. *(Click as phone goes dead)*

(Dolores is staring at her in disbelief)

DOLORES: You're not going to do it? Please say you're not going to do it.
MAGDA: Do what? What are you talking about?
DOLORES: He said contract. I heard him. O God, that means you will.
MAGDA: You knew about it? *(Silence)* Dolores, answer me.
DOLORES: Yes, yes, I've known all along.
MAGDA: What?!
DOLORES: I just kept it to myself.
MAGDA: You haven't said a word? Well, have you?
DOLORES: *(Miserably)* No.
MAGDA: Well, that was smart of you.
DOLORES: I'm sorry, Magda.
MAGDA: What put you on to it? When did you first know?

DOLORES: I think it was my birthday. That's when I first saw it. The day Victor went to Florida.

MAGDA: *(Sharply)* Don't try to be clever, Dolores.

DOLORES: And now you'll go away.

MAGDA: Do you think I'd stick around this joint with half a million bucks in my pocket?

DOLORES: But you'll take Dolores, won't you, Magda? You wouldn't go without me, would you?

MAGDA: Shut up, Dolores.

DOLORES: Magda, please. Magda, I'll kill myself.

MAGDA: God knows why the damn fools couldn't have got rid of him there and then, instead of having you walk in on a stiff.

(Magda sits thinking. Dolores' face changes from desperation, to puzzlement, to understanding, to a slow cunning. She looks at Magda triumphantly)

DOLORES: *(Slowly)* But, you see, you must take Dolores with you. She knows Lana. She made Lana. She's the only one who understands her.

MAGDA: Cut the Lana number right now.

DOLORES: O, no, I can't. Because there couldn't be a Lana without Dolores. *(Pause)* It's because of me she still lives. I keep her alive.

MAGDA: *(Slowly comprehending)* What are you trying to say, Dolores?

DOLORES: I'm glad Victor's... gone to Florida. He's much better out the way. But what happens when people start to wonder why he doesn't show? They'll start to ask questions.

MAGDA: They'll ask. But no one knows.

DOLORES: Dolores knows.

MAGDA: Dolores knows too much.

(Black-out)

ACT TWO
SCENE TEN

(New York. In the bar. A figure in Magda's clothes stands with her back to the audience as Heddy enters)

HEDDY: Magda, I've come to say 'goodbye'. I feel so completely wretched. I can't go on deceiving Dolores. Sneaking round behind her back. My self-respect is gone. I have to go away, to leave you. Even though it tears me apart. It's the only right thing to do.

(The figure turns to reveal not Magda but Dolores. She is smiling and her voice is like Magda's)

DOLORES: Dear Heddy, always such scrupulous principles. *(Heddy backs away in horror)* So you're off in pursuit of the truth, are you? Of great moral victories and ethical triumphs? We're going away too.

HEDDY: Dolores!

DOLORES: Yes, Dolores and I are going to Hollywood. We're going to create Lana together. The movie, you know. But of course you knew. Dolores told you, didn't she? And you told me. Now it's all settled. The contract and everything.

HEDDY: *(Aghast)* Dolores, you're crazy.

DOLORES: You weren't supposed to tell, Heddy, But it's O.K. You see, it was all meant to be. My whole life has led to this. Everything I've done, everything I've been, all leads to Lana. I'll be wonderful, won't I Heddy? *(Moves towards her)* Can you imagine the… accolades?

HEDDY: Dolores, for God's sake. Control yourself.

DOLORES: O, but you see, I have absolute control, Heddy.

HEDDY: *(Desperately)* Pull yourself together. Can't you see, you're just not yourself.

DOLORES: O, no, that's where you're wrong. For the first time in my life, I am truly myself.

(Black-out)

ACT TWO
SCENE ELEVEN

(London. Ella's flat, Dagmar and Kay are standing in front of an astonished Ella)

DAGMAR: You know too much. Far too much for someone of your inclinations. Well, what's it going to be, when it comes to the crunch? Reputation? Career? Or information? My comrade here would like it from your lips, wouldn't you?

KAY: From your lips, o yes, certainly would.

DAGMAR: Because she just can't believe it.

KAY: Nope, it's amazing. My luck's sure in today.

DAGMAR: She's anxious to learn about a… Guesthouse.

KAY: O, no, I'm not. Not any more. I'm having too much fun right here.

DAGMAR: *(Staring at her)* What? I don't understand.

ELLA: *(Laughing triumphantly)* Don't you? Your 'comrade' is an agent. *Our* side, sweetie, and on my payroll. Got yourself in a bit of a fix now, haven't you? You see, I sent her to get you.

DAGMAR: *(Looking from one to the other)* You sent her.

KAY: That's right. We were worried about you.

DAGMAR: About me? O, but it's not me. It's her. She's the bloody dike. Look, don't misunderstand what happened in the club...

ELLA: What happened in the club? Did you make a pass at her?

KAY: *(Proudly)* Yep, she did.

ELLA: After all your promises of everlasting love. You walk out of here...

KAY: Just the same as you did.

DAGMAR: What? You bastard. And I've been hating myself for doing this. Because of the way I feel about you... *(Stops suddenly and looks at Kay)*

ELLA: As I said she's working for me at the moment. And besides, she's one too.

DAGMAR: *(Still looking at Kay)* Are you absolutely sure?

KAY: Want to see a diploma?

ELLA: Anyway, why should you care? You're giving it all up, aren't you? Leaving the Service. 'Coming out'.... or are you?

(Dagmar backs away from her stare of growing suspicion)

DAGMAR: Ella, believe me, I didn't want to do it. It was an order from the top.

ELLA: How could you lie there beside me...

DAGMAR: You know it's impossible to refuse.

ELLA: You betrayed me!

DAGMAR: They wanted you checked. It's my job. *You* know. It's your job.

ELLA: It wouldn't have been very much longer. *(They look at each other)* So it's all been one big lie, right from the start.

DAGMAR: O no. It was never hard to desire you.

KAY: I can imagine. *(Throughout she sits and looks from one to the other)*

ELLA: *(Coldly)* Thanks. For nothing.

DAGMAR: What I didn't bargain for was falling in love with you.

KAY: O dear... It's going to be a weepie.

DAGMAR: Do you think I haven't been through hell.

ELLA: O, Dagmar.

KAY: Kleenex, anyone?

DAGMAR: I love you.

ELLA: Do you? Do you really?

KAY: And I was doing so well earlier on. Two propositions!

ELLA: *(Suddenly pushing Dagmar away)* You haven't made your report yet?

DAGMAR: No. I went to the club and got drunk. I just didn't know what to do. If I gave you a clean bill, said you were straight, and they already knew you weren't, then I'd be for the chop.

KAY: Yeah, save your own skin. That's the important thing.

ELLA: *(Turning on Kay)* What else could she do?

DAGMAR: That's right. Stop interfering.

ELLA: O, my poor Dagmar. How you must have suffered.

KAY: I hate to butt in...

ELLA: Then don't. *(To Dagmar)* But what will you tell them, so that you're clear of suspicion?

DAGMAR: I'll think of something. *(Takes Ella's hands)* Trust me.

KAY: *(Suddenly rubbing her nose)* I'd rather play baseball with a hand grenade.

ELLA: Let's think... There must be something...

KAY: *(To herself)* Geez, I don't know...

DAGMAR: That's it. Of course. I just don't know. I never ascertained one way or the other.

ELLA: *(Relieved and seductive)* In that case, I'd better make it absolutely clear to you.

DAGMAR: So now we can go on, the same as ever.

ELLA: Yes.

DAGMAR: As long as we're really careful. No one will ever know.

KAY: Sounds like a whole heap of fun!

ELLA: And we'll have each other.

KAY: Won't last. Nope. Know how many rides into the sunset wind up in my office, fighting over who gets to keep the saddle?

DAGMAR: Who asked you?

ELLA: Keep out of this.

KAY: O.K., O.K., I'm just telling you I wouldn't trust her, that's all.

DAGMAR: Now listen you...

ELLA: Why not?

KAY: I seen a lot of people in a jam, fighting for their lives, their freedom. They're sweating with fear. So they sing. Alright. But this dame gave me a three-part opera before the heat was on.

ELLA: *(Looking at Dagmar)* Is that so?

DAGMAR: I'd no idea who the hell she was. She could have been Head of Department for all I bloody knew. Don't look at me like that. I did what I had to do. If I hadn't, someone else would have done.

KAY: That's what the 'friendly witnesses' said at the hearings.

ELLA: *(Quietly to herself)* That's what the guards must have said at the camps.

DAGMAR: What I told you here tonight was the truth, I love you, Ella.

KAY: Good, because I taped it like you said.

DAGMAR: You did what?

KAY: Just like you asked me to.

DAGMAR: *(Feverishly)* Look, it was all a big joke, wasn't it, Ella? We were just playing a silly game because we knew we were on tape. That's right, isn't it, Ella?

KAY: That's not what it's going to sound like on this baby. *(Holds up tape recorder)*

DAGMAR: *(In desperation)* It was all *her* fault. *(Points to Ella)* She forced me into it. I didn't want to. She used her position of authority over me…

(Ella begins to laugh, then to cry. Kay puts an arm round her)

ELLA: Love is a cruel mistress. *(Looking at a silent Dagmar)* She can turn towards you a smile of promise that holds you captivated. *(Angrily at Dagmar)* But those full red lips are just painted onto a death's head!

KAY: I'm sorry. I thought it best you know.

ELLA: Who are you, anyway? What *are* you doing here?

KAY: *(Thoughtfully)* Good question. In 1955, I was a Private Eye working on a case.

ELLA: In 1955! And now?

KAY: I think I'm still trying to solve it.

ELLA: Aren't you a little late. Like three decades too late?

KAY: *(In alarm)* Too late? Geez, I hope not.

(Black-out)

ACT TWO
SCENE TWELVE

(New York. The sound of a shot. Hurrying feet. Lights up in bar)

HEDDY: Magda, don't go in there.

MAGDA: What's happened? I heard a shot. Let me by, will you?

HEDDY: It's Dolores. She's dead. Sit down, Magda. I'll deal with it.

MAGDA: Dead?

HEDDY: Suicide. The gun's still in her hand. She holding the picture of Lana. Magda, I'm sorry.

MAGDA: Yes.

HEDDY: But you can't blame yourself this time. If it's anyone's fault, it's mine. I didn't realise she'd gone over the edge. I guess the contract was the final straw.

MAGDA: *(Sharply)* Contract?

HEDDY: Yeah, you're getting it.

MAGDA: *You* knew about it?

HEDDY: She showed me the piece in Silver Screen the night of her birthday. About the auditions for the Lana movie. She knew you'd get the part automatically.

MAGDA: A contract for a movie!

HEDDY: It must have come as a terrible shock to her. Well, it did to me. You never told me you'd actually got it, Magda.

MAGDA: Hollywood are making a movie about Lana?

HEDDY: Well, yes. You knew, didn't you?

MAGDA: And she assumed I'd got the contract.

HEDDY: I don't understand. Haven't you?

MAGDA: Not yet.

HEDDY: Dolores was sure you were going to Hollywood.

MAGDA: O yes, I shall now. A movie of Lana. This is my chance. I'll be a star again. *(Exultantly)*

HEDDY: You don't sound very upset. About Dolores. Wasn't she important?

MAGDA: *(In a delicious dream of the future)* O, yes, she was important. She showed me Lana. I know just how to play her now. Every gesture, every inflection, every nuance, I have her here inside me. It's going to be the greatest movie Hollywood has ever made.

HEDDY: Is that what Dolores died for? A movie?

MAGDA: How many people can boast such an epitaph?

HEDDY: You'd use her death like that?

MAGDA: How many mean and meagre lives get the chance to end in such glory? Don't you think Dolores would be rather proud?

HEDDY: Do you ever love people for themselves? Must they always have a purpose for you?

MAGDA: Life is too short to love more than one person.

HEDDY: Yourself?

MAGDA: That's right.

HEDDY: You're a dangerous woman, Magda.

MAGDA: Because I put myself first? Because I don't lose myself in love, in what a woman's supposed to be good at? Instead I pursue what I know I'm good at.

HEDDY: But does it have to be so selfishly?

MAGDA: Both you and Dolores coiled your dreams around me like a snake. And now, because I refuse to be squeezed into submission by them, I am selfish.

HEDDY: Alright. But how the hell can you sit here and talk about a movie when your lover's dead in the next room? It's indecent.

MAGDA: I can see you would feel better if I fainted and screamed with grief, wouldn't you? That would be natural.

HEDDY: For God's sake, it would at least be human. The way you're acting now terrifies me. I just don't understand.

MAGDA: And you're afraid of what you don't understand. If I love, I must love with the right expressions of emotion. If I am unfaithful, it must be accompanied be the correct amount of guilt. And when I mourn, it must be in accordance with what is expected Otherwise I am an indecent woman. I am a dangerous woman. Because I upset the whole scheme of things.

(Kay enters at a gallop)

KAY: I'm back.

MAGDA: The cavalry.

KAY: Magda, are you O.K.?

MAGDA: I'm O.K.

KAY: Good. Heddy, you O.K.?

HEDDY: I'm O.K.

KAY: Good.

HEDDY: Dolores is dead.

KAY: Goo... What! Dolores. O my gosh. Dolores? But that doesn't figure.

HEDDY: In the office. She committed suicide.

KAY: Are you sure?

MAGDA: Well, the hole in her forehead didn't get there by accident.

KAY: *(Exiting)* Goddam! Goddam!!

HEDDY: *(Standing at Magda)* I never said the bullet went through her forehead.

MAGDA: Didn't you? I must have been thinking of Victor. I mean of how Dolores said she saw Victor.

KAY: *(Re-entering)* Nope, just as I thought. That wasn't no suicide. She was murdered.

MAGDA: Murdered? Nobody would want to kill Dolores.

KAY: You.

MAGDA: What?

KAY: The bullet was meant for you. She was wearing your dress, right? That cute little green number? Right. From the back she'd've looked just like you. Easy enough mistake to make, huh?

HEDDY: Yes. Easy enough. But, look, she wasn't shot in the back.

KAY: So she turned, they fired, then it was too late. Hold this. *(Hands Magda the gun)*

HEDDY: If it is murder, should you be handling that?

KAY: Huh? The gun? O you can see—no prints. Except one set. Dolores' presumably. Another suspicious circumstance. Any others have been carefully wiped off. Clever, you see. This guy has murdered before.

MAGDA: But this is just too melodramatic. Who'd want to kill either...

KAY: Hold the gun in front of you and point it at your forehead.

MAGDA: Are you crazy?

KAY: It's O.K. It's not loaded any more. *(Magda reluctantly obeys)* Comfortable?

MAGDA: Of course I'm not comfortable. This thing's giving me the creeps and my arm's aching.

KAY: Exactly. If you're going to shoot yourself in the head, you do it like this, right? *(Takes gun and holds it to the side of her head)* At the temple. That way you don't have to see the gun, just close your eyes, squeeze. All over. Think, Magda. There's someone who's got it in for you. Maybe someone who still thinks you're too communist. Or too anti-communist.

MAGDA: Or someone who simply didn't like my last picture. Come on.

87

KAY: I know it's hard to credit, Magda. But this world is a nasty place and someone, somewhere has put a contract out on you. (*Exits musing*)

HEDDY: Contract? Contract out? Just needs that extra little word and it changes the meaning completely. Is that what happened to Dolores? You didn't know about the Lana contract. You said so. So why was she so sure you did? Dolores got it wrong, didn't she? She thought she heard you talking about a film contract. But it was really a contract to kill.

MAGDA: I want to be left alone now.

HEDDY: Why? So you can 'mourn' in your own way? Or so you can clear up your traces after you? The families only put the contract out on someone important. It must be a big job. Wait a minute, the press-cutting. Pedroza. Why?

MAGDA: A certain government agency pays a lot of money for the 'eradication' of its enemies.

HEDDY: Victor too?

MAGDA: The bastard thought he could run out on me with all the dough.

HEDDY: So that's it. And Dolores...?

MAGDA: Knew too much. And so do you, my little Heddy. (*Raises gun*)

KAY: (*Entering unobserved*) Like I said, it's not loaded. Drop it, sister.

MAGDA: (*Trapped*) You can't prove a thing. I'll deny it all. Nobody will believe you.

HEDDY: She's right.

KAY: But I got it all down on tape. Listen. (*Rewinds*) I left the room purposely, because I knew you would incriminate yourself. Murderers always do. (*Presses it to 'on' proudly and settles back. Silence. She fiddles. Only buzzing and incoherent voices result. Madga laughs*)

MAGDA: Well, that's evidence a jury can't ignore.

KAY: Goddam, I thought I'd figured it out. What's the matter with this machine?

MAGDA: Now if you'll excuse me, I've a flight booked for L.A. tonight. And there's something I must do before I go. (*Exits*)

KAY: (*Agape*) She's gone. She's escaping justice.

HEDDY: It looks like it.

KAY: Hell, that's all wrong.

HEDDY: (*Laughs bitterly*) Of course, in every good detective story, the villain pays for her crime.

KAY: That's right. Society's got to abide by certain rules...

HEDDY: But Magda has never been bound by any of them. (*Starts to laugh*) I talk about kicking the system, worry about it, debate endlessly the whys and wherefores, and Magda just goes ahead and does it. (*Stops laughing and looks yearningly after her*) And we all love her.

(*Black-out and spot up on Magda before the picture of Lana, singing "Looking at Lana" song*)

HEDDY: *(Staring after Magda)* They just walked out the door. Magda and all my dreams.

KAY: Put the two together and you wind up with the same thing in the end.

HEDDY: What do you mean?

KAY: Magda is the great Hollywood dream made flesh.

HEDDY: Magda's real.

KAY: Uh uh. Like all dreams, she seduced you.

HEDDY: The great Hollywood dream. Is that all desire is?

KAY: All this one was.

HEDDY: No... She was a woman who knew what she wanted and took it.

KAY: And killed three people doing it. There are other ways of getting what you want, that don't involve so many fatalities. Come on, wake up, Heddy. There's a whole world out there—out here—that's missed you. You got work to do.

HEDDY: Reporters are ten cents a dozen.

KAY: Not ones like you. You're special. And not just as a reporter either. *(A pause)* Well, I guess you probably need to be alone right now, so I'll scram. But... if you need anyone to help pick up the pieces and... uh... stick them back together again, I'm pretty good at that.

HEDDY: *(Looking at her for the first time)* Thanks Kay. I appreciate it. But just give me a rain-check on that, will you? Right now there's something I want to tear to pieces. A little letter on my editor's desk. *(She takes her arm and looks at her a moment before going)* You take care now. *(She exits)*

KAY: Ciao.

ACT TWO
SCENE THIRTEEN

(Ella's flat. A knock at the door, Ella opens it)

ELLA: Tea? Coffee? Sugar?

MONIKA: *(Laughing)* No, none of those.

ELLA: By what were you drawn? The sound of the wireless? Of... my friend?

MONIKA: By the silence. And by you. *(They look at each other)*

ELLA: Come in.

MONIKA: And by hope.

ELLA: You look for hope in the hopeless. You know my lover has gone. And she never really cared much at all.

MONIKA: In her own way she did, maybe.

ELLA: Only as far as Department regulations permitted.

MONIKA: And you? Didn't you go so far and no more? If you embrace an ideology that denies love, you must accept the consequences. But now I do not see hopelessness. I see a woman who has looked deep into her heart, examined it meticulously bit by bit, as only someone like you could do.

ELLA: Are you laughing at me?

MONIKA: No, no. Of that I would not dream. Such a thing as you do takes great courage.

ELLA: Yes, I have looked into my heart. And been sickened by what I saw.

MONIKA: Then you will change it.

ELLA: I'm giving up my job.

MONIKA: I know.

ELLA: How can you know that? I've just decided myself.

MONIKA: Yes, it is in your eyes. Excitement. A new fire.

ELLA: *(A wry laugh)* What you see is terror. And the thing is I have no illusions about what good my action will do. It's just a small, insignificant drop in the ocean.

MONIKA: Of what is the ocean made up, if not small drops? You are a woman of strong convictions, and you will fight for them.

ELLA: I never questioned before. Never had cause to, I suppose. My childhood was modelled strictly on the Empire line. One held a certain position in the community. With that went certain values, duties, loyalties that one took for granted. Everything else was ignored. Uncomfortable social realities, one's own sexual preferences, all remained securely under lock and key. No, I'm not afraid of fighting. But I am of failing.

MONIKA: O, you will fail. Often. But then you try again. And so we inch forward, separately and together. The defeats are as important as the victories. They teach us that we cannot stop struggling. We must stretch society to fit the human spirit as it grows and expands. And when it seems we have gone back instead of forwards, we must remind ourselves that the strength of the backlash is a measure of our progress.

ELLA: I feel so fragile.

MONIKA: Strength grows as you use it.

ELLA: Why do you have such faith in me? Yesterday I was prepared to send people like your daughter to... Guesthouses. Don't I disgust you?

MONIKA: We are similar in some ways, you and I. *(A pause, then slowly)* You see, in the camp... I wasn't... a prisoner.

ELLA: Not a prisoner... but... but then you must have been...

MONIKA: A guard. Yes.

ELLA: *(Shrinking away)* My God.

MONIKA: *(Unable to look at her)* We knew they would come for us that day. I ran into the streets. I had no idea where I was going. Only to get away, to stay free a little bit longer. In an alleyway I fell over the body of a girl. She wore the uniform of the Party Youth. I took her clothes from her and put them on. I took her identity and gave it to myself. I was very young, of prime child-bearing age. My duty to my Fuehrer would have been to reproduce little S.S. officers for the Reich, or be a guard in the camps. I chose the latter.

ELLA: What a thing to live with.

MONIKA: *(Harshly)* No, do not give me pity. That I cannot bear. At the time, to survive was everything. So many times since, death has seemed gentler.

ELLA: Beside yours, my choice seems to small. Almost of no importance.

MONIKA: Every choice we make is important. We make the world what it is.

ELLA: I think I should like to be alone now.

MONIKA: I taint the air. I know that. I see the horror in your eyes.

ELLA: That's not it. I just need to… absorb everything. Tomorrow…

MONIKA: *(Leaving)* Perhaps. We shall see.

ELLA: I need time, that's all. I, of all people, have no right to condemn. Is that why you told me? Why you chose me?

MONIKA: That is my own, selfish reason, yes. But there are others.

ELLA: I do want to be your friend, very much… if I can.

MONIKA: I know. You are capable of great love. And what you love you will love with passion. Somewhere deep down the ice begins to melt and will become a flood. Goodnight, Miss Ford.

THE END

SONG LYRICS

PULP

I want to see my life
In print for a change
In a book with a glossy cover
Don't you know
I'd be drawn by the
Glamour
Of your paperback folds
Hypnotically sold on your
Soft-cover charms

1) I want the thrill
    Of a tale that's told
    Romantically
    About the girls who love the girls

The ones who do not care for boys
The ones who got away

2) I want to thumb
   Through the pages of a different life
   And discover
   Everything I'd always known
   But never seen
   Lined in black and white

CHORUS (x2)
   Oooh addicted to Pulp
   Oooh you got me hooked
   Pulp is the fix sold
   On the bookstands
   Of your dreams
   On the line, everytime
   Girl meets girl

3) I want the pleasure
   Of a tale that's told
   Passionately
   Where the horse-backed heroine
   Saves Beauty from the Beast
   And she doesn't die

4) I want the tale of a
   Private eye
   Who's tough as nails
   Who gets a kick
   From drinking rye,
   Who gambles all
   And gets the girls—
   And is not a dick

TIME

I'm numb
Dull to the core
My eyes are steel bars
See only walls
Dead ends and ice

I'm outrun and void
Scarred by the silence I've made
The city shades
My concrete eyes
As you and I hold hands
Do we ever know for sure
We share the same moment

I gather the parts of me
I'll wait forever
Longing for change
The twilight hour
Is a restless gift
Between the day and our dreams
There are layers
Between our words
Boundless immeasurable
Strands we recall
Those we lose with the dead
Eons behind
But also eons ahead

I sense a gap
Between reality and me
A light year scans the time
Across the wasteland of our intimacy
I am reflected
In the rhythm of neon
Fragmented by its pulse
There is somewhere further on
I want to be
Someone further on
I wish to be

ODD GIRL OUT

We can tell
At a glance
The cut of your suit
And lay of lapel
Betrays you
By the calls you receive
And the looks you give

When you think you're unseen
We are watching

The solace you seek
Your sapphic embrace
Is known to us
Curled in the arms of a foreign power
Your desire
Strips away disguise
The confession begins

You will be used
Made to talk
They want your secrets
Every detail
Every heart beat
Every bargain embrace
You'll give our facts
And our figures
Our discs and our digits
Plans diagrams
You'll give the game away

Tales of the state
Slip from your lips
You are open to abuse
That'll tear at your soul
Till your breath is cold
A social disease
Your kiss risks all
A judas in our midst

LOOKING AT LANA

Silver roccoco
Frames a glimpse
Of someone she knew
There was a time
She held that gaze
A phase
In the haze of her mind
When that smile tugged and prised

The laughter of her life
All trace of you
Is finely woven
With my loss
A re-occuring dream
You linger
Never away for long
Dipping delightfully
Close to her beat

And when the film was over
And the credits rolled
You were the name and face she gave
To all that was out of her reach
An elusive
Fantasy of you

Lana what prompted you to stir me now
Why clutch my naked throat with your call
Lana you've got her
So leave me now
Lana
Leave me now

DANCE WITH A DIFFERENCE

We are together
Relative strangers
Caught in the limelight
Of the cellar bar
We play a tough game
The dice is loaded
There is no referee
Who's keeping score?

We're all gamblers and loners
Oddballs and queers
We run a hard race
We fight the same fears
It's a long bumpy ride
And the winner's fixed
The odds are uneven
But we still take the risk

Raise your glass
To a dance with a difference
Down here we live
In paradise

I drink a toast:...
To our uncle who was always curious: His eyes were always
watching
To our aunt who moralised: Her tone it patronised
To our cousin who was embarrassed: Her face it was always flushed
To our brother who thought it was funny: His laughter was cruel
To our sister: she was scared: Her nerve it seemed to crack
To our father he kept silent: A knot that was never untied
To our mother who never approved: Like a door that was always
locked

I raise a toast to you all
The women who love and recognise
Their sisters at the bar
Raise your glass
To a dance with a difference
Down here we live
In paradise

TROUBLE (BAR SONG)

They call me trouble
And heartache
Sorrow is my deadly game
I'm a walking live wire
I even give danger a bad name

I'm a powder keg
An unlit fuse
I've got a mouth like a tunnel
It will swallow you whole
A tongue
Like a viper
I will poison your soul
One look from me
Your blood will turn cold

Trouble
They call me trouble

GIRLS I ADVISE YOU

(Nevydavaj. Traditional Czech)

Girls I advise you, don't marry not yet.
Once they get married girls grumble and fret.
Unmarried girls, dear, can do as they please.
Free as a bird or a fish that roams, that roams the deep seas.

Weaving her garland of flow'rs and green ferns,
Dreaming and longing, oh how her heart burns!
Some time that morning she'll see her loved lad.
Don't marry—marriage is dreary, girl, is dreary and sad.

Pulp. Hilary Ramsden (Kay). Photo: Anita Corbin.

Pulp. Left to right: Jane Boston (Magda) and Jude Winter (Heddy). Photo: Anita Corbin.

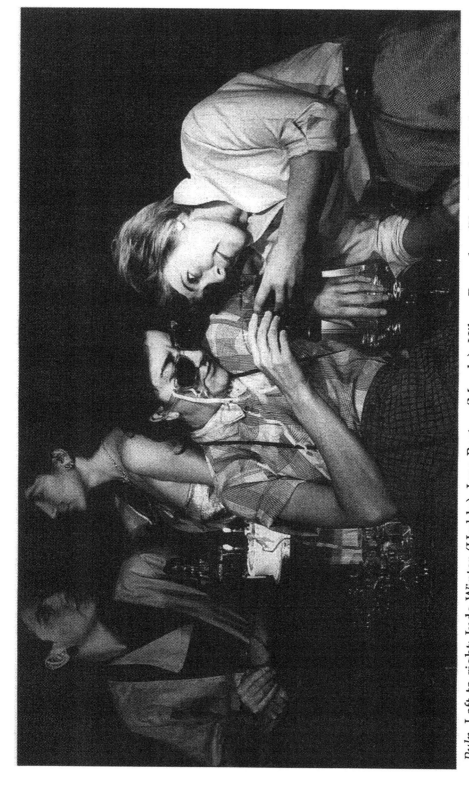

Pulp. Left to right: Jude Winter (Heddy), Jane Boston (Magda), Hilary Ramsden (Kay), Tasha Fairbanks (Dolores). Photo: Anita Corbin.

Pulp. Tasha Fairbanks (Dolores). Photo: Anita Corbin.

NOW WASH YOUR HANDS, PLEASE

by
TASHA FAIRBANKS

FROM DISCUSSION AND WORKSHOPS WITH SIREN THEATRE
COMPANY

SONG LYRICS: JANE BOSTON AND TASHA FAIRBANKS
COMPOSITION: JANE BOSTON AND JUDE WINTER

FIRST PERFORMED AT THE NIGHTINGALE, BRIGHTON, 1984

THE COMPANY

P. R.: JUDE WINTER
BERT AND POLLY (AND DUMMY MANIPULATION): TASHA
FAIRBANKS
PHYLLIS AND BERT'S MUM: HILARY RAMSDEN

MUSICIAN AND ADMINISTRATION: JANE BOSTON
DESIGNER AND TECHNICIAN: DEBRA TRETHEWEY

THE PLAY WAS DIRECTED BY SUE SAUNDERS

PERFORMANCE NOTES

The action takes place on an intercity passenger train that is secretly carrying nuclear waste. The play, however, is NOT about the nuclear industry. Waste, like the train, is only used as a metaphor.

The time is 1984, the mid-Thatcher years and the watershed of the miners' strike. Confident and cynical, P. R. hardly bothers to maintain the illusion of consensus, but is, himself, taken in by the illusion of three dummies, posing as the very nuclear family he is busy promoting.

THE CHARACTERS

THE REAL (OR SORT OF) ONES
P. R.—A Thatcher and Saatchi right-hand man.
Bert—A working-class British Rail guard, with a secret.
Phyllis—A middle-class physicist.
Polly—A working-class, lesbian feminist revolutionary, who just happens to be an ace ventriloquist as well.
The Ghost of Bert's Mum—The ghost of Bert's Mum.

THE DUMMIES/NUCLEAR FAMILY
Mrs—A Family-sized Persil packet with a smiley face on.
Uri—Her son, a ventriloquist dummy.
Pluto—Their dog.

SET DESIGN

The set was a giant wooden horseshoe shape with a lid that descended at the end of the play, to reveal itself as a toilet seat. The acting took place in, on and around the set.

THE MUSIC

The rock songs served as an alienation device, disrupting the narrative while the actors took up instruments. The lyrics often underscore the particular political message by use of an extended metaphor, as in *White Out*.

The song and dance numbers, (*Them and Us* and *Singing in the Acid Rain*), were a vaudeville-style continuance of the action, emphasising the 'up yours' frivolity of those in power.

NOW WASH YOUR HANDS, PLEASE

ACT ONE

P. R.: Everything running smoothly?

BERT: *(Takes out watch)* Yes, sir. We depart in 4 minutes 32$\frac{1}{2}$ seconds precisely.

P. R.: Good, good. We've got some Physics chap from base to keep an eye on 'you know what'. So look out for him will you?

BERT: Some Physics chap? And I take it he is to be welcomed aboard?

P. R.: Most certainly.

BERT: *(Takes out note book)* "Welcome aboard", just jot that down in case of confusion. Only I'm also keeping a sharp eye out for burly women with short hair and sleeping bags.

P. R.: Good. Well, you know what to do if you spot any of those.

BERT: *(He spits on his hands, rubs them and, taking hold of P. R., whirls him round so he is pinioned in a painful judo hold).*

P. R.: Ow, let go of me, you idiot. Have you gone mad?

BERT: *(Rubbing him down concernedly)* Beg pardon sir. Only a little demonstration.

P. R.: Don't use that word.

BERT: No, sorry, sir, I forgot.

P. R.: And if there's any trouble, on your head be it.

BERT: *(Proudly lifts hat and displays a gun)* That's exactly where it is, sir.

P. R.: *(Looking round nervously)* Put it away, you fool. This is England, not a military state.

BERT: No, sir?

P. R.: Now I'm going off to see if our Family has turned up. It'll be a right muck-up if they haven't.

(They freeze, enter Phyllis)

PHYLLIS: It has been said, though not scientifically proven, that my lectures on Einstein are turgid, unimaginative and give Einstein a bad name. And that, furthermore, I'm a boring old fart. Hmmmm. The central problem must lie in communication, because to my mind there's nothing more exciting. Just think—that enormous leap forwards from Newton's theory of the world as static and compartmentalised to the Quantum theory—energy in constant motion, effecting universal change. Isn't it quite thrilling? But people are still clinging to outmoded ideas when we're living in a Quantum Age, with all its endless possibilities. It's a crisis of perception. Yes, very good Phyllis. And that's how I must gear my lecture. But how? If only one could communicate dynamic, revolutionary concepts that question the very nature of what we believe is natural in a catchy jingle.

P. R.: *(Sings)* "This is the Age of the Train". *(Phyllis freezes)* We all know the sad story of the Labour Party election defeat. What went wrong, we ask ourselves. Well, in attempting a critical analysis, let me borrow a few well-known lines from that great British Institution, British Rail—"Now wash your hands, please". You see, the Labour Party went into the elections with the grime and, let's face it, the shit of old, outmoded policies all over one hand and the steaming turds of the Militant Tendencies on the other. They came out onto the hustings without having flushed their differences down the pan, and with their trousers still round their ankles.

Carrying on the analogy, half of them seemed to be in the front and the others in the rear of a train that split in two different directions. The question was "Who had the Party Ticket?" With this dilemma to deal with, there could be no clear signal to the voters. Neither portion could strike a communication chord in the electorate. And that's the way we plan to keep it.

Stranded in the sideings of one of the few branch lines that hadn't thrown out their Parliamentary candidate, with a Buffet car selling powdered tea at 21 pence a cup, they could only watch helplessly as the Thatcher 125 Inter-City Express hurtled by. A smiling Jimmy Saville waves and offers a Student Railcard to anyone who can get a place in Further Education. The Tory high-speed express is streamlined, comfy, and sells powdered tea at 30 pence a cup, and the fact that no one can afford it makes it all the more appealing.

BERT: The train now standing at Platform One will call at Gloucester, Double Gloucester, Cheshire, Cheddar, Wensleydale, Derby and Lymeswold.

PHYLLIS: But I don't want to go to any of those places.

BERT: Hard cheese.

PHYLLIS: Then I'm on the wrong train?

BERT: Not if you want to go to Gloucester, Double Gloucester…

PHYLLIS: I don't. But I've searched everywhere, there aren't any other trains in the station.

BERT: There's one in the sidings.

PHYLLIS: Where's that going?

BERT: Nowhere. *(He blows his whistle)* Mind the doors, please.

PHYLLIS: *(Pulling down the window)* The train's moving. We're leaving the station behind.

BERT: In this train, Madam, it is dangerous to stick your neck out.

PHYLLIS: But what should I do?

BERT: That is your decision.

PHYLLIS: How can I make a sensible decision when you won't give me any information? *(Bert ignores her)* Guard, where does this train stop?

BERT: The train terminates at the terminus.

PHYLLIS: But where can I get off?

BERT: I could tell you.

PHYLLIS: Listen, I want to change. I have to make connections, and you are not being helpful.

BERT: There is nothing in the bye-laws that requires me to be helpful. *(Consulting bye-laws)*

PHYLLIS: In fact, you are being very obstructive.

BERT: Move along now.

PHYLLIS: And my suitcase is still back in Left Luggage.

BERT: *(Swinging round)* Centre Left, Militant Trot Left, or completely off the bleedin' rocker Left?

PHYLLIS: I don't know. What does it matter?

BERT: Tickets, please.

PHYLLIS: Think Phyllis. Now what would Einstein have done? The only way to move a dense mass…

BERT: Have your tickets ready, please.

PHYLLIS: Of great volume is to launch oneself at it with tremendous velocity. On guard… *(She prepares to charge)*

P. R.: Having trouble? No sweat. *(Shakes her hand)* Percy P. Rations, but just call me P. R. Perhaps I can be of assistance. What's the prob? Slight rumble on the rails? Would you care to make a complaint?

PHYLLIS: Yes, I would. Everytime I try to explain my position I come up against a barrier of meaningless opposition that I just can't get through.

BERT: Not without a ticket, you can't.

P. R.: *(Writes it down)* What was that? Barrier of meaningless…?

PHYLLIS: Opposition.

P. R.: Opp-os-ition. Right, I'll make sure this receives the appropriate attention. *(Puts it behind his back and proceeds to tear it up)* Every protest and complaint is given careful consideration.

PHYLLIS: But, you see, I'm on the wrong train. I'm going in a totally different direction from where I want to end up.

P. R.: Such a common cry from the heart nowadays, don't you think?

PHYLLIS: I'm supposed to deliver a lecture on molecular physics…

P. R.: Ahhh. *(Suddenly alert and looking round)* How fascinating. One of our new technologists. This is the age of the brain, what. Phew, it's alright, no need to keep up the pretence, we're quite alone. I do apologise, you see I had expected a man. You see, it's a delicate situation, this is the first passenger train to have a 'you know what', a uh hum, receptacle for waste.

PHYLLIS: *(Aside)* How very coy. *(Aloud)* But how did one manage before?

P. R.: Straight into the Irish Sea.

PHYLLIS: From here? Extraordinary. Must have been a lot of near misses.

P. R.: Yes, 'fraid so.

PHYLLIS: The sheer inconvenience. And if it's dangerous to stick your *neck* out of the window, you must have taken your life in your hands to maintain that position.

P. R.: Yes, jolly sensitive area. Everything was fine, though till a load of Commie agents started stirring it up.

PHYLLIS: How foul of them.

P. R.: 'Course it got everywhere then. They shoved it all into the public eye. Nasty business.

PHYLLIS: I can imagine.

P. R.: So we had to clean up, fast. By the way, you are properly briefed?

PHYLLIS: That is none of your business.

P. R.: Ah, but it is.

PHYLLIS: How dare you.

P. R.: Look, it's just because we can't afford any slips here.

PHYLLIS: I realise you expected a man, but I do not want to hear your archaic views on petticoat scientists.

P. R.: Eh? O come now, Madam, I'm completely unprejudiced. Why, some of my best friends have friends who know someone who knows a lady scientist. Besides, we encourage everyone who's eligible to be scientists these days. We want our universities, eh,… the remaining University, to be full of them. The Arts was always a hotbed of revolution. Sociology seethes with interfering do-gooders. And as for History, well, the sooner we can get it all onto computer, the better for all of us.

PHYLLIS: Why?

P. R.: Because any history that isn't on computer just won't exist, will it? No tradition of Class Struggle. No harking back to Chartists and General Strikes. Yes, class divisions will be a thing of the past. Peoples' memories fade fast, but the floppy disc stays on forever. No, we like our Scientists. No seething with unrest over their molecules, eh? Too much money to be had for that sort of thing. Now, most important thing—stay near the 'you know what', and don't communicate with anyone. Bye.

PHYLLIS: *(Alone)* Odious little man. What a ridiculous conversation. Who on earth can he think I am? Don't communicate with anyone indeed. What rot. That's exactly what I started out to do. Though goodness knows how I get off this train. Wait till it stops in, where was it? Double Gloucester, then make a connection, I suppose. Meanwhile Phyllis old girl, you may as well get to grips with the original problem—the lecture. Trouble is, I don't think I have the common touch. What I need is to get chatting to some ordinary folk, practise my theories on them.

(As she has been talking to herself there has been a new arrival. A young woman enters with a suitcase and flops down. She kicks off high-heeled shoes, takes off a

long blonde wig and scratches her cropped hair. She looks at her watch, then out of the window)

POLLY: Fifteen minutes to zero hour. I s'pose I'd better get them out in case someone starts nosing around.

(She opens the suitcase and brings out three dummies. One is dressed as a boy, Uri, another is a large piece of foam with the face of a Persil packet, Mrs, and the third is a dog, Pluto)

Who could suspect such a nice little family as you two. Three, sorry Pluto.

PHYLLIS: Cooee. Anyone there?

POLLY: O bloody hell, not already. *(She quickly puts on her wig, jams her feet into the shoes and puts her hands behind the boy dummy and the foam dummy, on either side of her and ventriloquises)*

MRS *(Persil Packet)*: Sorry, dear, all the seats are taken. Try next door.

URI *(Boy Dummy)*: We got a dangerous dog in here.

PLUTO *(Fluffy dog)*: Woof.

URI: Pluto always bites strangers when she's pregnant. Specially when she's just about to drop 'em.

PLUTO: Woof.

MRS: Yes, doesn't see why she should be the only one to suffer.

PHYLLIS: O there seems to be heaps of room. Hello, Pluto.

URI: She tears their throats out.

PHYLLIS: Nice doggie. There. You *know* I've got a Standing Order to the R.S.P.C.A, don't you? Yes. Phew, I'm quite puffed. You know there's the most yawning gap between the First Class carriages and these ones. Had to do a long jump to get here.

MRS: Well, as you're here now, pull up a broken spring and sit down.

PHYLLIS: O thanks. Awfully kind. I won't be a jiff, actually. I just wanted a little chat. You see, I'm preparing a lecture on... O, by the way, I'm Phyllis. I'm a physicist.

POLLY: Of course, one of you lot had to be on the train.

PHYLLIS: How strange. You're the second person who seems to have expected me. There was some ghastly official who got very personal and then stuck me in a carriage next to the 'you know what'.

MRS: In case of an accident, you mean?

PHYLLIS: I suppose so.

URI: And what if you have one, Four Eyes, what you going to do then?

MRS: Uri, that's rude.

PLUTO: Woof.

PHYLLIS: *(Aside)* I say, these people are very earthy. I suppose one must reply in the same vein. *(Aloud)* Well, I suppose I'd just mop up the shit and keep mum.

MRS: Not tell a soul.
PHYLLIS: Certainly not.
POLLY: (Aside) Typical.
PHYLLIS: Eh, haven't I seen your face somewhere before, Mrs...?
MRS: Have you, dear?
PHYLLIS: On a television commerical. But it was more of a squarer face, rectangular even.
MRS: No, it wouldn't have been me, dear. Not on the telly.
PHYLLIS: 'S funny, I could have sworn.
POLLY: You just can't trust the evidence of your own eyes these days.
PHYLLIS: Now isn't that extraordinary. That's exactly what my lecture's about. I say, as we're all sitting here so cosy, do you think I might try out a little of my lecture on you? I'm sure you don't mind being used as guinea pigs, do you?
POLLY: 'Course not. We're used to it.
MRS: Sit up straight, Uri. You're going to be lectured to. As usual.

(But Irony is wasted on Phyllis)

PHYLLIS: Jolly kind. Now this is Einstein's General Theory of Relativity.
URI: We don't like our relatives.
PHYLLIS: (Sternly) Now you mustn't start confusing it with his Special Theory of Relativity.
MRS: We wouldn't dream of it.
PHYLLIS: Now, Einstein's theory shows us that we do not see the world as it really is.

(She pauses for dramatic effect)

POLLY: (Low) You certainly don't!
PHYLLIS: The rational human mind has very limited perspectives and regardless of how the world really is, the mind sees only what it's been taught to see.
MRS: My, my, you wouldn't credit it. Isn't that amazing, Uri? (Straight at Phyllis) So you don't see what's there at all?
PHYLLIS: No, no. We unconsciously try to superimpose these beliefs on the real world, even when what we see positively contradicts them.
MRS: Makes you wonder if anything's what it seems.
POLLY: Or what they say it is.
PHYLLIS: Exactly. It's a crisis of perception.
POLLY: (Bitterly) Yes, very clever. Congratulations on your discovery.
PHYLLIS: Lord no. It wasn't me. It was Einstein. (To Mrs) And did you see it clearly?
MRS: O, we saw it clearly, didn't we?

PLUTO: Woof.

POLLY: It's very clear what she's up to. She's not as stupid as she looks.

MRS: You're not sure yet, Pol. You could have got her wrong.

PHYLLIS: *(Meditatively)* Yes, and the trouble is, it's a trap that's very difficult to escape, even when you're aware of it.

POLLY: See what I mean. She's sussed me right away.

MRS: She's got such an honest face.

POLLY: So did Attila the Hun, probably. She's a scientist, what else would she be doing on the train, taking care of any leaks and making sure no one knows about them. She's just been playing games with us. She knew all along, I bet.

MRS: She could just be what she seems, Pol.

POLLY: No, they sent her to unnerve me, Make me do something stupid and give the others away. Can't afford to take chances.

URI: What you going to do, Pol? Throttle her and chuck her out the window?

MRS: Ooh, Uri, no. She might get stuck half way. Then what would we say?

URI: She was trying to catch another train. Ha ha.

PLUTO: Woof.

POLLY: Shut up, you lot, this is serious. Oh, what am I doing talking to a load of dummies? She's just waiting for the guards to come and arrest me. I won't even have time to give the comrades the signal. What shall I do? Even though we're hurtling along at 125 miles an hour, I could fling open the door and, clutching my favourite picture of Rosa Luxemborg, throw myself... my four selves, out the train. No, I will not resort to the tactics of the bourgeois sensationalist film-maker. Escapist capitalist pseudo art shall not become revolutionary strategy. Besides, I'm a coward. I don't want to end up a jam doughnut on a telegraph pole.

PHYLLIS: *(Coming abruptly out of her reflections)* Would you like to hear about Quantum Mechanics?

(Enter an irritated P. R.)

P. R.: Ah, here you are. *(Sotto voce)* You know you really must stick to your post, eh, your compartment. *(Aloud)* This is the carriage especially reserved for the Family.

PHYLLIS: O but we were having such a good chinwag about the Theory of Relativity, weren't we?

POLLY: Yes, o yes. It was fascinating.

P. R.: Mmm, but we do like to see people comfortably seated in their own particular part of the train. Too much toing and froing in the communicating corridors might just rock the train. And we wouldn't want that, would we?

POLLY: No, might get a sudden lurch to the Left.

P. R.: (*He looks up suspiciously but she smiles back sweetly*) A word with you in private if I may.

PHYLLIS: Well, bye, lovely to meet you. I'm sure I'll see you again. Then I can give you the low-down on Quantum Mechanics.

P. R.: That will be a treat for them, I'm sure.

(*Exit*)

POLLY: (*Huge sigh*) She can't be for real.

MRS: No, she can't can she? (*Polly looks at her in surprise*)

P. R.: (*Leading Phyllis away*) I really wouldn't bother, if I were you. It just goes in one ear and out the other with them. You see, the great mass of the populat...

PHYLLIS: Mass? Ah, $E = MC^2$, what? Jolly old Quantum Theory. Mass equals energy in constant interrelating motion.

P. R.: That is what we most definitely discourage. No, it's very kind of you to take time with them. But, to be quite honest, anyone who believes half the announcements we put out needs their heads examined. You should see them scuttling about after non-existent trains. What a giggle, some of them end up shunted into the knackers yard.

PHYLLIS: (*Coldly*) Yes, that's exactly what happened to me.

P. R.: Ah, yes. Unfortunate that. But we could hardly lay down the blue carpet or put up signs saying "Scientific chappie this way", could we now?

PHYLLIS: You seem to have a very irresponsible attitude towards the welfare of your passengers.

P. R.: Well Fare? Well Fare? Rings a bell. Probably one of those 'Super-Survivor Deals' we go in for to confuse everyone. That's another lark. There's hundreds of them and the really funny thing (*P. R. is pissing himself*) is the rules are different for every one of them. Confuses the hell out of me.

PHYLLIS: (*Coldly*) I suppose this only applies to second-class passengers?

P. R.: Good Lord, yes. Executive class wouldn't stand for it. (*Puts friendly arm around her.*) Correct me if I'm wrong, but I think that somewhere along the line you've inherited what we call in the trade—a conscience. Thought so. Take my advice, get rid of it. Won't get you any favours up top, and that lot in there won't thank you for it. They'll milk you for all they can get, then say 'Up yours'. Let me explain. (*Singing. Phyllis joining in, hesitantly at first, but getting carried away by the end*)

> You see, there's them and there's us
> The burnt bit at the bottom and the upper crust
> To each the task unto which (s)he's born,
> For us it's brain, for them it's brawn.
> Talk of Equality, talk through your arse
> There'll always be First and Second Class.

We're democratic at the poll,
But once we're in, we're in control.

See here, there's us and there's them,
Skimmed milk and the "crème de la crème"
The trick's not to put it quite that way,
Or when you say "heel", they'll not obey.
Convince them all opportunity's there
Then they can't complain and say "it's not fair".
Quite contrary to what they say
You can fool all the people just about every day.

P. R.: There, that should set you straight. Don't mention it. Any time.

PHYLLIS: But, I still feel…

P. R.: Don't. You're a Scientist, you just concentrate on your little atoms. We'll take care of the soft 'sells'! Ha ha. In other words, you do the fission, we've got the vision. Ha ha. Well, I must go and see about our *(Bends close laughing)* Nuclear Family. Ha ha ha ha ha.

(The White Out song)
(Enter a smiling P. R. into the family compartment narrowly missing seeing Polly signalling with a torch out of the window)

POLLY: O shit, not him again. You'd almost think there was a conspiracy against this conspiracy.

P. R.: Ah, don't tell me. I'd recognise your acceptable faces anywhere— you're travelling on your half-price Family Railcards.

URI: No we're not. We're travelling free, like you said we could.

MRS: We couldn't have afforded to come, otherwise.

P. R.: But you could if you'd saved your Persil tops.

URI: No, we couldn't.

P. R.: O yes, you could.

URI: O no, we couldn't.

P. R.: *(Grabs Uri by the throat)* O yes, you could, get it? You little bugger, the Press are going to come and interview you soon. And they're going to ask you about all the little Child Benefits…

URI: Like what?

P. R.: *(Produces balloon and snips off the end of it)* Like this.

URI: *(Howling)* Why'd you do that?

P. R.: Protect it from inflation. And you're going to tell them about all those nice Family Income colour supplements *(Hands him comics)* you've received since you stepped over the wonderful 125 Tax threshold. You see, we stood on a platform of no more poverty. Poverty's still standing on the platform and we've left it far behind on our 125 Express.

(Polly takes the balloon and makes a farting noise through it. P. R. looks furiously at Uri)

MRS: Uri!

URI: Wasn't me.

P. R.: Uri? What a nice name. After the first astronaut?

MRS: No, Uri's short for Uranium. He was born at Windscale.

PLUTO: Woof.

MRS: And that's Pluto, short for Plutonium. And this is Polly...

P. R.: Short for...

MRS: Her age.

P. R.: Mmm, I think we'll leave out the names when the Press come, and say you're from... eh... Sellafield. Yes, nice and obscure. And, remember, you're all taking this golden opportunity Family Away Day while Daddy's at work.

POLLY: No, we left Daddy ages ago 'cos he was a nasty, boring, boozy old shithead who beat us up. Ow, Mummy kicked me.

MRS: Polly, I told you not to wash our dirty linen in public. We're on this nice man's poster.

P. R.: That's right. If you can't keep it clean, at least keep it in the family. Privatisation is next to Godliness.

URI: There's a lot of things that'd come out in the wash if we wanted to tell the newspapers.

P. R.: Listen, you little brat...

MRS: You mustn't mind him, sir. He's not very well. But don't worry, they're having the time of their half-lives.

P. R.: Good, good. I knew I could rely on the co-operation of you and your eh, model nuclear family to promote our model nucl... eh, new railway.

URI: Why should we?

P. R.: *(As though patting his head, P. R. grabs Uri's hair)* Because we built the 125 to serve your needs, and so you're going to help us flog it to the general public, right?

MRS: Thank the nice man for his presents, Uri.

P. R.: O it's nothing.

POLLY: No, what's a few freebies for giving him a white wash? *(P. R. glares at her suspiciously, but she smiles innocently back at him)*

URI: Is that all we get?

P. R.: Unless you start collecting more Persil packet tops.

URI: Here, I got a present for you. Show him, Pol.

P. R.: *(Taking them)* O, eh, thank you.

MRS: That was a kind gesture, Uri.

P. R.: Yes, what a nice little chap. Eh, what are they exactly?

URI: Two bits of the Cumbrian coastline. *(P. R. drops them and flees)* It's alright. They've both been washed in the Irish Sea.

P. R.: Bert, Bert.

BERT: Coming, sir.

P. R.: Bert, what did I ask those idiots at H. Q. to find me?

BERT: *(Thinking)* A normal, radiant nuclear family, sir.

P. R.: And what did they come up with? An irradiated bunch of oddbods whose only claim to nuclear is that they come from Sellafield. I mean, if I hadn't known what a family looked like... I've never seen a more abnormal lot in all my life.

BERT: Must have been a hard job to find one nowadays. You just gotta look at the statistics...

P. R.: I never look at statistics unless they agree with me. I wasn't asking for the earth, Bert. I just wanted your everyday, standard, listen to the Archers on Sunday morning, add Bisto to your gravy, nuclear family.

BERT: But that's just it, sir. There's not many of them left.

P. R.: Are you trying to tell me the family as we know and love it is a myth?

BERT: No, sir, it just doesn't exist.

P. R.: But Bert... *(Suddenly he breaks into stirring song)*

TOGETHER: "There'll always be a family
No matter what they say
Excuse for the Family Wage
To keep out Equal Pay;
A shrine for moral virtues
A blind for inequalities,
The scapegoat for society's wrongs
A haven for the casualties.

There'll always be a Family
For each man knows its role,
To succour him and comfort him
On his return from the dole:
It gives him pride of purpose,
The continuance of his line,
And as we'll give him sod all else
The Family suits us fine".

P. R.: Spirits up, Bert. As long as we believe it exists, they will. *(Phyllis comes rushing up to them)*

BERT: O blimey, not her again.

PHYLLIS: I say, the train's slowing down. Are we approaching Double Gloucester?

BERT: *(Consulting his watch)* Nowhere near.

PHYLLIS: But we're definitely slowing down.

P. R.: It may *seem* like the train's slowing down, but in reality it's just countryside moving forward. Einstein's Theory of Relativity. O we're well-versed in that.

BERT: She's right, sir. We've definitely lost power.

PHYLLIS: There. It's stopped. I told you so.

P. R.: Only temporarily. All out. Everybody out. (*For the rest of the speech he is alone*) This is an emergency. We must all pull together till the train gathers speed. Do not panic, anyone. This is not a major crisis. All the signs say that we shall soon be on our way again. But remember, every man, woman and child of you, we are all in this train together.

PHYLLIS: (*Offstage, grunting and groaning*) *Most* of us are outside pulling.

P. R.: Each must pull his weight. We have one common aim—it is only the full co-operation of you all that will get us moving ahead. Only the willingness of you, the passengers, to sacrifice that little snooze you'd planned in the corner seat, or the can of lager in the Buffet car, that and that alone will ensure that this great train of ours will regain its speed— with safety, with humanity, with honour, with dignity and freedom.

PHYLLIS: I say, look here, I'm quite ready to do my bit and pull together with the rest, but, really, I do think it's a bit much if all of us poor so and sos out there are working like billyo and you're just sitting in here jollying us along, then having a zizz. Especially as I didn't want to be on this bally train anyway.

P. R.: But you shouldn't have been pulling. Leave that to the masses... eh, and simply masses of people out there. You should remain inside, making frequent visits to the 'you know what'.

PHYLLIS: (*Aside*) The man's obsessed. (*Aloud*) Look here, I haven't got the runs, you know.

P. R.: (*Leading her by the arm*) No, no. Absolutely no need to run. Too suspicious anyway. Just a casual walk past now and then. (*He demonstrates whistling suspiciously and glancing round furtively; Bert emerges to the sound of a flushing loo, looking equally as furtive as P. R. They see each other and both jump*)

P. R.: Bert. What on earth are you doing?

BERT: (*Whispers*) Little leak, sir.

P. R.: Couldn't you have waited? We need everyone available out there pulling.

BERT: No sir, no. Little leakage seems to have occurred.

P. R.: And it's gone into there. Ah, how apt in its own way. The waste of both activities mingling and merging in the continuing cycle of the process and reprocess of life and death. (*To Phyllis*) You'll mop this up, won't you?

PHYLLIS: I most certainly will not.

P. R.: O come now, that's your job. We couldn't do it.

BERT: Not capable.

P. R.: Wouldn't know where to start. O and if you can't clean it all up, make sure it runs into the *Second* Class carriages.

PHYLLIS: Well, of all... I shall use a rude word. Just because I'm a woman you think I have a natural gift for mopping up the shit, do you?

(But P. R. and Bert are deep in conversation)

BERT: No sir. Information leak.

P. R.: What!! To the Press. I knew it. They've got wind of the fact that our nuclear family's a bit on the odd side. Probably know the boy's on his last legs. Damn that little bugger. What was he doing rolling round on the beach at Sellafield for, anyway? Couldn't he just have walked round upright, wearing protective boots and gloves, like our chappies? Why couldn't he have used a geiger counter? They're on sale in all the Souvenir Kiosks. You know, Bert, these people contract incurable diseases on purpose, to spite us.

BERT: Yes sir, but...

P. R.: Think, Bert. What can we do?

BERT: *(Proudly)* Don't you worry, sir. I'm thinking.

PHYLLIS: Well, I'm going back to my lecture notes.

P. R.: Lecture. Lecture. I've got it. How's this? He's an exceptionally bright kid from a struggling but happy family, so we are providing on-the-spot education and medical attention, because we are a caring train. Where's the First Aid kit?

BERT: You dismantled it, sir. Said people should bloody well provide their own. Gave bits of it away to your mates, at a price.

P. R.: Nonsense, Bert, I never had any intention of dismantling the First Aid box. Well, give me what's left, anyway.

PHYLLIS: *(Entering or unfreezing)* This train's not moving an inch. What are you going to do about it?

P. R.: *(Ordering Bert)* Uncouple the last ten carriages. *(Taped murmurs of objection. To audience)* It gives me great sorrow to have to do this, Ladies and Gentlemen. But while most of you have been very good, responsible passengers, pulling with all your might on this St. Crispin's day, uhhum, there are others, a minority, yes, but I fear, a large minority, who do not fit this category. I mention no names, but look around you, worthy passengers, see who they are by their faces.

BERT: *(Moving amongst the audience)* I can spot them a mile off.

P. R.: The lazy, the bone idle, the ones who are only on this train because they have so-called relatives who got them on with a Family Rail Card, the ones who've only paid half fare while you've paid the full whack. They are travelling at your expense. *And* preventing the train from running smoothly. I ask you, Ladies and Gentlemen, is it fair? Is it really fair? That you should be paying for their joy ride? Don't you feel you're being had, while they're laughing all the way to the terminus? I put it to you, Ladies and Gentlemen, should we let them get away with it? *(Look at the smirks on their faces)*, or should we streamline our train for those of us who really do deserve our seats? I knew you'd co-operate. Get rid of the last ten carriages, Bert. Soon we'll have a complete return to power. Everything under control.

PHYLLIS: I say, isn't that a bit heartless, leaving the poor devils stranded like that?

P. R.: Think of your children.

PHYLLIS: I haven't got any children.

P. R.: Well, think of your cat then. Think of your poodle. These people are taking the Pedigree Chum from its poor little mouth.

PHYLLIS: *(To herself)* I fail to see the logic in any of this. *(Bert and P. R. begin to speak in the rhythm of a train starting and gathering speed)*

BERT: Eh, sir, did you feel that bump further back? It felt like a jolting motion on the track.

P. R.: You mean?

BERT: Yes, I mean it might mean we're back in business.

P. R.: Jolly good, knew we would, indeed.

BERT: Start slow, but here we go, we're gaining speed.

P. R.: That'll show the wets we know what's what.

BERT: In spite of that delay. *(Consults watch)*

P. R.: We made them play it our way shouldn't be late.

P. R.: Now we're rid of that freight.

TOGETHER: We're in a jolly fine State. Whoooo. Whoooo.

BERT: Thought we'd had it there, sir. Phew. Do you think it was the work of extremists?

P. R.: Could be, but no matter, Bert, these things are sent to try us. Besides, from every little skirmish we learn something to our tactical advantage, what? *(To Phyllis)* There, what did I tell you. We're on our way again. *(Calls)* Everyone back in their seats immediately. You all know your places, please remain in them. *(To Phyllis)* Now, I have rather a special job for you. You can forget your post for a while and be private tutor to our scientific whizz kid in there. We'll let the Press see what lengths we go to fool everyone... eh, to furnish the under-privileged youth of this train with an education. Eh, by the way, if you're thinking this means a pay rise, 4.5% is the absolute limit. Well, I shall go in now with my First Aid box and make sure he doesn't kick the bucket before the Press see him.

PHYLLIS: But he's not a whizz kid, anyone can see that. I can't make a silk purse out of a sow's ear.

P. R.: But between us, we can make a sow's ear look for all the world like a silk purse. That's what matters on this train we like to make sure everyone receives equal opportunity, so we are about to provide this young man with his very own Science Tutor. And here she is. A very warm welcome, please for... *(Phyllis appears)*

POLLY: O no. Not her.

PHYLLIS: Hello again. I'd just like to say how wonderful it is to be here and to have this opportunity to try out my lecture.

P. R.: *(Looking closely at Uri)* Mmm. Before I get the Press, I'll just check his ticker, make sure he's still clinically alive.

PHYLLIS: I say, he does look rather sleepy, should I go on?

P. R.: O yes, it's just intense concentration. Doesn't want to miss a word. *(P. R. puts his ear next to Uri's heart. Uri bites his ear hard and holds on)* Owww, you little brute.

MRS: Ahh, he's taken a real fancy to you, hasn't he? That's nice. Mind your fillings, Uri. *(P. R. thankfully escapes as Phyllis takes centre stage)*

PHYLLIS: In the early years of the Twentieth Century, physicists began to realise, very slowly, that the world wasn't, as they'd always imagined, just one awfully jolly big machine, that busied itself, working away according to the Laws of Motion, and that could be broken down into its constituent parts. Nor was Matter, the material world, made up of isolated, compartmentalised, building blocks. But of teeny weeny dynamic particles that inter-related, and could only be understood through their mutual inter-dependence. You see, all living things are multi-levelled structures, each level consisting of smaller sub-systems, which are wholes in regards to their parts and parts in respect to the larger wholes. But you can soon see that the idea of the wholes become immaterial because this one is part of this one, and that connected to that, and this one to this one and so on and on. Atoms are made up of particles, but these are not static substances. No, that is not what we see. What we see are dynamic patterns continually changing into one another—the continuous dance of Energy. No, this is not an illusion—patterns of matter and patterns of mind are reflections of one another. *(Freezes in lecture pose)*

P. R.: *(Pacing up and down, to himself)* Gentlemen of the Press, you see on this train the fruits of our labours, the appreciation of all our great efforts— happy, smiling, radiating faces, well-cushioned bums, luggage racks that don't send cases crashing down on your head while you're doing the crossword. Well , write it down, write it down, I'm dictating.

BERT: Sir, sir.

P. R.: Go away, Bert. Can't you see I'm preparing my address to the Press. Must give our nuclear family some good copy.

BERT: That's just it, sir. You didn't stop to hear me out. The leak wasn't about the family, it was. *(Whispers and points to audience)*

P. R.: What! *(Bert goes out into audience as P. R. addresses them)* Anyone here from G.C.H.Q., M.O.D., M.I.5., M.I.6., M1 Junction 13 roadworks and contra-flow system...

(Meanwhile Bert is interrogating members of the audience as to how they knew about the show that night. When he finds someone who has been told by someone else, he brings that person out)

So you had the information in your possession that tonight there'd be some lefty frolics here, some anti-establishment antics, some political fun and games, yes? And what did you do with that information? Speak up, let everyone hear. You leaked it. In the certain knowledge that it would lead to more people being exposed to this crap. *(With sudden charm)* By the way, what colour are my eyes? *(Gets answer)* There you are. Do you realise that's classified information? You're a threat to national security. Can't keep anything to her/himself. An inveterate leaker. In front of witnesses. I'll deal with you later. And don't expect the Press to make you into a bloody hero/ine. They're still shitting themselves about the last one.

BERT: You'd better get yourself a good lawyer, my girl/lad, 'cos you're not going to like Holloway/Parkhurst.

P. R.: O, by the way, while you're in there, seeing as you're a trendy liberal, if you'd like to make a documentary about the injustices and abuses of the Prison System and Legal Process and what not, let me know. We can provide you with all the necessary equipment. *(He rubs his hands)* Right, good, everything under control? Capital! Well, I reckon they'll think twice now before passing on subversive information again.

BERT: Yes sir. Nothing like a show of unprovoked force to preserve law and order.

P. R.: Reminds me, Bert, of that inspiring poem by the great MacGregor:

"Not a word sworn
Not a stone tossed,
Not a riot shield rippled,
When into the picket lines
Rode the 600."

BERT: Beautiful, sir, beautiful.

P. R.: From the Hansard Book of English Worst.

BERT: Very moving. Eh, sorry to wrench your mind from memories of past glories, sir, but what should we do about 'her'?

P. R.: Her?

BERT: Her in there what's teaching that brat science.

P. R.: O leave them to it. Can't be doing any harm.

BERT: I wouldn't know, sir. Never had the opportunity myself.

P. R.: The Press will still want to interview them at some point.

BERT: Huh, intellectuals. She can't even read a British Rail Timetable.

P. R.: The little sod's probably nodded off and the women are nattering about knitting patterns.

BERT: *(Singing)* But, sir, that woman's nuts.

P. R.: Of course, 'cos she's not us. Bert, there's us and there's them. Just thank your stars we're not the same.

TOGETHER *(Sing)*: Be they smart or be they thick
We'll never know what makes them tick,
Some are delicious, but quite capricious,
Some are boring, some downright vicious,
Some feed your ego, some make you sick,
All in all, we take our pick.
Give her what she deserves
And we foretell
Whatever the mileage
She'll serve you well.
There's nothing better after
A day with the fellers,
To lay your head down
On her breast and tell her
She's the mother we don't have in us
To heal the wounds, wipe out the pus.
So long as she does it, there's no fuss
That's why there's them, and there's us.

(Meanwhile Phyllis is still in full spate. Mrs, Pluto, and Uri are 'dozing', Polly is listening)

URI: Zzzzzzz. *(Snore)*

PLUTO: Woof, zzzzzz, woof.

PHYLLIS: When quantum physics was finally accepted, it was a great Scientific Revolution.

P. R.: *(En passant)* Revolution! *(Spasm)* Don't use that word. It has revolutionary overtones.

PHYLLIS: Because, you see, some of the Physics community realised the impossibility of grafting the new, dynamic ideas onto old, outworn structures. They felt deeply threatened and afraid.

POLLY: I bet.

PHYLLIS: They were in control and had an awful lot invested in the old physics.

POLLY: Ain't it always the same old story.

PHYLLIS: And, of course, how could the new physicists even begin to explain their ideas using the old, inadequate scientific language?

POLLY: *(Alert)* And?

PHYLLIS: Well, what other language could they speak and be heard in?

POLLY: So? Did they find a way?

PHYLLIS: O yes.

POLLY: What was it?

PHYLLIS: Mathematics.

POLLY: (Sarcastically aside) O great. Sisters, brothers, comrades, now is the time for XY^3 = the square root of Z–T.

PHYLLIS: Well, that was the lecture. How was I?

POLLY: (Unenthusiastically) Great, just great.

PHYLLIS: Thanks awfully. You know you are kind. Eh, your mother and Uri seem to have gone to sleep.

POLLY: (Sharply) Yes.

PHYLLIS: What a shame. And it was so good. Quite my best. I feel ever so chuffed. Thanks again.

POLLY: That's O.K., go ahead and use us any time, Atomic theories. Atomic tests. That's what we're here for.

PHYLLIS: (Uncomfortably) Eh, I should have thought we'd be at Double Gloucester by now, wouldn't you?

POLLY: Why? What's happening there?

PHYLLIS: That's where I'm going to change.

POLLY: Into what?

PHYLLIS: No, change. Make a connection. I just hope I'll get there in time. (Looking at watch)

POLLY: Look, how can anyone know so much and not see what's happening in front of their eyes?

PHYLLIS: O, you'd like to hear the Theory of Relativity again, well...

POLLY: I just don't believe you.

PHYLLIS: Ah, now you're beginning to ask the same questions that Einstein started with. You see you've grasped the idea, that's the main thing. (Polly suddenly pulls off her wig) Good Lord.

POLLY: Yeah, I'm not what I seem. (Pushes over Mrs and Uri) Nor are they. Nor is this whole bloody train, if only you could see. If only you could make some connections.

PHYLLIS: I don't know what you're talking about.

POLLY: O don't you? Well, for a start there's the small matter of the nuclear waste you're looking after on the train.

PHYLLIS: Ah, now that is a common mistake to assume that anyone who studies physics produces nucle... On the train! I'm looking after!

POLLY: The 'You know what' as you put it.

PHYLLIS: So that's what he meant. Look, this has all been a terrible mistake, it's got nothing at all to do with me...

POLLY: 'Course not. You just make the big discoveries, win the Nobel prizes, then wash your hands of it all.

PHYLLIS: I merely do my job. What they choose to do with it is...

POLLY: Your affair.

PHYLLIS: I take care of the fission...

POLLY: They make the decisions. That's a nice little equation for you. Why don't you put it into mathematics? Scientist minus responsibility equals politicians' power infinitely recurring. *(Phyllis is, for once, speechless)*

POLLY: *(Moving towards her)* I'm not taking any chances with you. I'm going to knock you out, tie you up and put you in that suitcase.

PHYLLIS: O no you're not, young lady. *(She adroitly grapples Polly to the ground and sits on her)*

POLLY: Ow, ow, get off me.

PHYLLIS: You will remain there till *I* decide to let you go. There's no point wriggling, I've done this many times before to Professor Blimski in the lab. Whenever he's made indecent suggestions about experimenting with my electromagnetic poles. He's at least 18 stone, so don't expect me to be intimidated by a young hooligan.

POLLY: I'm not a hooligan. We just want a chance to get people to listen to our ideas. Ow.

PHYLLIS: What ideas?

POLLY: I suppose it comes as a surprise to you that we've got ideas too.

PHYLLIS: Who are these 'we' you keep talking about?

POLLY: Has it escaped your notice that there's First and Second Class on this train?

PHYLLIS: Certainly not. Nearly broke my ankle jumping across the gap.

POLLY: Better be careful going back then. It gets wider every time.

PHYLLIS: Does it? Good Lord, do you think I'll make it?

POLLY: Dunno. I don't even have one-way mobility, let alone two.

PHYLLIS: Mmm, anyway, you were telling me about these ideas of yours. *(She settles herself ready)*

POLLY: Comfy, are you?

PHYLLIS: Thanks. Well? I'm listening.

POLLY: Congratulations. Must be hard for you.

PHYLLIS: I'll pass that by.

POLLY: How kind. If you think I'm going to tell you about oppression with your arse on top of me...

PHYLLIS: I'm sorry, but I shan't get up till I'm quite satisfied you are not a dangerous terrorist.

POLLY: You can relax. They're all in places like the White House. Yeah, I am dangerous. But not in the way you mean. My ideas are dangerous to your smug, complacent way of life.

PHYLLIS: I see, and you think you've come up with all the answers.

POLLY: No. We're starting to re-phrase the questions.

PHYLLIS: Mmm. So society's not up to scratch. But be specific, what part are you talking about?

POLLY: *You* ask me that. It's not just certain isolated issues. That's the way they try and make us see it, so they keep us split up from each other, stop us seeing the connections.

PHYLLIS: Prevent dynamic inter-relations?

POLLY: That's right. The way we see the world is all wrong.

PHYLLIS: Back to the old crisis of perception.

POLLY: We want to turn the world upside down, so people can see some of the possibilities, once we get away from this one-track way of thinking. But we're up against Poxy Percy...

PHYLLIS: Newton.

POLLY: And all the power and machinery of his 125. That's why we stopped it.

PHYLLIS: (Shifting her weight abruptly) You stopped the train back there? Sorry. Forgot you're not Professor Blimski. But that was jolly irresponsible. What about the poor people in the last ten carriages.

POLLY: He was planning to unlink them, anyway, while no one was looking.

PHYLLIS: So you did it for him?

POLLY: At least the way we did it, people knew what was happening and that it could happen to them. That's the first step. They're making connections.

PHYLLIS: Not till we reach Double Gloucester.

POLLY: Will you shut up about Double Gloucester?

PHYLLIS: You deliberately stranded those poor...

POLLY: We didn't. He did.

PHYLLIS: But he had no alternative. If the train jolly-well stops and has to be bump-started, naturally some of the ballast...

POLLY: O ballast are we? Did you see the First class get out and push.

PHYLLIS: I did.

POLLY: Were any of them left stranded in the middle of nowhere? And what about the people who couldn't afford a ticket to get on? Have any of us had any choice where we're actually going?

PHYLLIS: My first words to the guard.

POLLY: But once people in the Second Class really know what's happening, there'll be a spontaneous uprising of the proletariat to form a new kind of life, built on humanity.

PHYLLIS: ...honour, dignity and freedom.

POLLY: How did...?

PHYLLIS: Poxy Percy's words exactly.

POLLY: That little rat.

PHYLLIS: With large teeth, in a big mouth. And I'm afraid he's swiped the words right out of yours for his own theories. Quite a problem. (She heaves herself up)

POLLY: (Getting up) I'm sure you'll think of a mathematical equation. Think of us when you get off at Double Gloucester.

PHYLLIS: Will you shut up about Double Gloucester. Polly, will you tell me more?

POLLY: Why should I waste my breath on you? I've been fucked over by your sort too often.

PHYLLIS: I wouldn't do that.

POLLY: How do I know I won't get it right back in my face.

PHYLLIS: You don't. You'll have to take a chance on me. But the only way you are going to change things is by communicating to people, helping them make connections. *(Pauses. Polly sits down)*

POLLY: Alright. But only if you can keep your mouth shut long enough.

INTERVAL

ACT TWO

(Owls Only song begins Act two. Black-out)

(P. R. is sitting as though asleep. Bert enters anxiously, a half-eaten apple in his hand)

BERT: Sir, sir. *(No response)* Mr P. R. sir. *(No response. Bert looks regretfully at the unfinished apple, then drops it on P. R.'s head)*

P. R.: *(Jumping)* What the hell do you think you're doing, bonking me on the head like that?

BERT: Sorry, sir. Wouldn't have done it if it was not for the gravity of the situation. I had to wake you up.

P. R.: I was not asleep, Bert. I was merely pondering the greatness of this machine of ours. *(With pride)* This 125 Inter-City Express. Or rather, this 125 Inter-Bureaucratic muddle of inadequately funded, mutually hostile Urban Borough Councils and unelected, Government-appointed quangos Express.

BERT: Yes. Eh, sir...

P. R.: In fact, Bert, I have just had mystical vision, as on the road to Emmaus...

BERT: Lymeswolde, sir.

P. R.: ...of an even bigger train. Twice as big, twice as fast. No, five, ten, twenty, a hundred times. Growth, Bert, unimpeded, unrestrained growth, like cancer cells—multiplying, bursting, thrusting out and destroying all the weaker tissue. Think, Bert, a new giant-size 125, pistons pulsating into the far beyond...

BERT: *(Grumbling)* Huh, big enough now. Get sore feet as it is, up and down clipping tickets all day...

P. R.: Think of the power of such a brute. Casting off all excess baggage, crushing whatever lay in its track.

BERT: Ah now, that's just what I was coming to...

P. R.: Think of it, Bert. Why we could have a 125 that stretched from Euston to Aberdeen.

BERT: I'm thinking sir. But what I thought was, if it stretched from Euston to Aberdeen, then the people what got on at Euston would have to walk to Aberdeen.

P. R.: You know Bert, you're the type who would've put the kybosh on Hannibal crossing the Alps with 2000 elephants, by telling him there was a funicular leaving in half an hour and thirty seconds precisely.

BERT: Yes sir. Thank you, sir. Sir, before you start talking about the train growing any more, I think I should warn you that the track ceases 500 yards ahead.

P. R.: What!!

BERT: Yes sir, we've run out of sleepers.

P. R.: Well? They could lay more down, couldn't they?

BERT: Wood, sir.

P. R.: Don't presume to teach me my grammar, Bert. They could, can, must, will.

BERT: No, sir, wood. W-ho-ho-dee.

P. R.: No wood?

BERT: No, sir. On account of the uncontrolled hemission of Sulphur Dioxide.

P. R.: *She* mission, Bert. Never let it be said we are sexist. Nonsense, nothing to do with sulphur dioxide, told them all so at that knees-up we went to in Bavaria. Told 'em not to take it so seriously.

BERT: It was a grand number we did for them, wasn't it? (*Strains of "Singing in the Rain" are audible*)

P. R.: Yes, it was. I was Fred and you were Ginger.

BERT: No, I was Ginger and you were Gene.

P. R.: Ah yes, I remember it well.

(*They start an old dance routine. P. R. at times puts up the umbrella, Bert pours the rain over it with a watering can. Sometimes he gets the timing wrong and the brolly goes down as he pours. High jinks ensue*)

TOGETHER: (*Singing*) Singing in the acid rain
Breathing in (*Cough*) and quickly out again
What a choking feeling
Those chimneys are smoking again.
I'm laughing at clouds that stretch across the skies
The oak turns to ash as it withers and dies.
Those yellow clouds chase
Every leaf from its place
The forests are bare

All the birds gone without a trace
But we'll never admit
It's us who emit
The sulphur dioxide in acid rain

Yes, we're singing and chancing acid rain.

P. R.: Now where were we?

BERT: Sleepers, sir.

P. R.: Mmm. And how many will we need to get us to Lymeswolde?

BERT: About 7 million, sir.

P. R.: And how many unemployed do we have at the moment?

BERT: Officially, sir? About three million, seven hundred and forty two.

P. R.: And unofficially?

BERT: Seven million.

P. R.: Ah, the sheer beauty of mathematics.

BERT: Sir! You can't mean... You couldn't be thinking of...

P. R.: Yes, Bert. That's exactly what I'm thinking of. Tough problems call for tough solutions. After all, sleeping is what the unemployed do most of the time. *(To audience)* Come now, this will just enable them to do it for the benefit of the great British way of Rail.

BERT: There'll be trouble. They won't take this lying down.

P. R.: Rubbish. It's an apprenticeship, Youth Training Scheme... training, get it?

BERT: *(Unhappily)* Yes sir.

P. R.: ... work experience, job satisfaction, gaining a good track record in industry... you can word it how you like.

BERT: But, sir, isn't this going a bit too far?

P. R.: Only as far as Lymeswolde.

BERT: But it's never been done before.

P. R.: Nonsense. In the last two World Whoop ups, we laid them down for the German tanks to run over, least this time it's a British train. Well, alright, just in case someone creates a hoohah, here's a White Paper on it. *(Getting out loo roll and writing on it)* "According to traditional practice, all unemployed persons shall, henceforth and notwithstanding, but lying prone on their stomachs, be employed as Government railway sleepers." Howzat?

BERT: But it's never been practice on the Railways. *(As he speaks, P. R. scribbles on the loo roll, pulling out more and more sheets that Bert gets himself tangled and wound up in)*

P. R.: 'Course it hasn't. The whole purpose of any Government White Paper is to make any totally new and outrageous scheme sound like it's been knocking around as traditional practice for yonks. Otherwise it wouldn't be worth the paper it's written on. Might as well just use it to wipe your arse. *(There's a sudden jolt)* Ah, I'd say they've laid the first assignment of sleepers.

BERT: *(Stumbling)* Bit bumpy, sir. Ouch, that must have hurt someone.

P. R.: They'll soon settle into the new job. *(Calls out)* In a democratic train, we are pledged to support all those who wish to go about their normal and lawful business. So carry on down there, you're doing a capital job, and the Government is right behind… eh, on top of you. You know, Bert, I almost envy them. No responsibilities, nothing to do but lie there.

(Exits thoughtfully. Bert paces, alone with his conscience)

BERT: Perhaps he's right after all. Give them a feeling of purpose in life, bit of self-respect, a place in the community. But yet… *(As Bert speaks the ghost of his mum appears in white, or black. Bert is still tangled in loo roll. They see each other and start!)*

MUM'S GHOST: Bert? Is that you? I haven't got me glasses.

BERT: Mum!

MUM'S GHOST: What you doing in all that white stuff? I thought thee were a ghost.

BERT: No, mum. 'Tis you who is the ghost. The ghost of mine own mother, died on a picket line, come back to haunt me. Oooohhh.

MUM'S GHOST: Stop dithering, Bert. The hour is almost come when I to sulphurous and tormenting flames must render up myself.

BERT: But, mum, you've already been cremated once. O… o, no… you mean… to hell?

MUM'S GHOST: No to Ravenscraig blast furnace. If you shut thy face a minute, I'll tell thee why.

BERT: Speak, Mother. Why hast thou returned?

MUM'S GHOST: I am thy Mother's Spirit, doomed to walk the night And by day confined t' heavenly steelworks in the sky, Till the foul crimes committed in my day on earth are purged away.

BERT: And where's Dad?

MUM'S GHOST: Thy Father's having talks on't new wage settlement with St. Peter for the H.U.M.

BERT: H.U.M.?

MUM'S GHOST: Heavenly Union of Mineworkers. They provide the coal for the furnaces of Hell, into which all capitalists and their minions descend.

BERT: God!

MUM'S GHOST: She's staying out of the negotiations. But, list, Bert, O list, if ever thou did'st thy dear Mother love.

BERT: O mummy.

MUM'S GHOST: Revenge this foul and unnatural murder.

BERT: Murder? But they told me you'd thrown yourself repeatedly at a police baton.

MUM'S GHOST: Aye, murder most foul. I mean the infernal butchery of t' Trade Union Movement, and t' smashing of t' class. 'Twas given out by right-wing press that we in front of colour tellies slept, while murderers smuggled in two weapons, laws of '80 and '82, to destroy our rights. All lies. We struggled. 'Twas T.U.C. did nowt, the craven, fawning pawns of Marguerite. Too little too late, 'twas allus same with them. But, Bert, biggest con. was Miners' fight. Government waited behind very thick blue line and rejoiced to see miner 'gainst miner, steelman 'gainst miner. Rejoicing, aye, 'cos now they could blame death of works and pits on us pickets, after they'd already plotted it. But what choice did Miners have? To fight together for t' class or be picked off one by one?

BERT: But they only wanted rid of twenty mines.

MUM'S GHOST: Idiot. It was the beginning of t' end. Nulcear they always meant to go. No Miners championing class struggle. Just arse-licking, universitied technocrats, plus endless plutonium to fuel their wars, and the threat of terrorists nicking it as excuse for the biggest load of armed fuzz in history. Nuclear power gave them power, endless power, to run their train as always on the backs of the workers.

BERT: No, mum, it's on the backs of the unemployed now.

MUM'S GHOST: And now you're on t' other side. To think I bred a traitor t' class. Who'd believe thee were my flesh and blood, mine own daughter?

BERT: Sshh, mum, not that. Don't tell them that, please, I'm a man now.

MUM'S GHOST: Masquerading as a man, you mean. And for what?

BERT: To get a bleeding job. And I'll tell you something else, being a man makes you feel different, see the world different. You see it from up, looking down, 'stead of the other way round. People treat you different. They don't say "Hello darling, like your tits". No, you got some say, some authority.

MUM'S GHOST: And what are you using it for? To smash t' union.

BERT: So? What has it ever done for me? Or you, for that matter?

MUM'S GHOST: Hold thy treacherous tongue, daughter.

BERT: Where was the union when you got arthritis and lost your packing job to young Betsy Parker? Where was the union when Aunt Sal got by-passed for promotion 35 years running to blokes who'd only just left school? Where was it when they reclassified Gran's job so they could keep her on half as much as the men? And when they closed the day nurseries, where was it? And when there weren't no jobs for women left at all?

MUM'S GHOST: Women, women, women. I'm talking about t' struggle of the working class. If the class wins, women win. We'd see the benefits soon enough, I know that.

BERT: Well, I don't. They had enough opportunities to show willing.

MUM'S GHOST: O thou scab of the earth, I'll listen to thy whining no longer.

BERT: But mum, what else could I do? No work, and a 10 year waiting-list for part-time jobs with rotten pay. I didn't want to give up and have a baby like all me mates, just to feel I was doing something, and to get enough Welfare to live on.

MUM'S GHOST: Some girls managed quite nicely *and* decently selling their milk tokens on the Black Market. At least they weren't willing skivvies for t' ruling class. Look at thee in that uniform. 'Tis unnatural. No daughter of mine art thou. *(Turns to go)*

BERT: *(Trying to bar her way)* Mum, mummy, don't go, please. I got myself a job, didn't I? Don't that count for nothing? And they never guessed. Ha ha. Pulled a fast one on them there, didn't I? Makes you laugh, don't it. *(Desperately)* Mum, aren't you a little bit proud of me? Say you are—just for once. Here, don't I look smart? You used to like me in my school uniform. Mum. *(Mum passes)* At least I'm not a sleeper!

MUM'S GHOST: *(Turning before she exits)* Vengeance is what I want. Avenge the class, or my curse be on thee for ever.

(Enter P. R. with drinks tray)

P. R.: Bert, whatever's the matter? You look as though you've seen a ghost.

BERT: Ghost, sir? Me? No. No ghost, sir. Been no ghost here or I'd've seen it, if there had been one. Which I didn't. So there wasn't. And even if it was here... which it wasn't it's gone now. At least, it would've gone, if it had been here in the first place. Which it wasn't. If you catch my meaning.

P. R.: Ye-es.

MUM'S GHOST: *(Off)* Before train whistles twice, you shall deny me thrice.

P. R.: *(Who hasn't heard)* Well, I've just had a little toddle along the train and everything seems to be running smoothly. Second class seem to be enjoying themselves in their own quaint, little way. I'd say we deserve a drink, old chap. What say you? Good wheeze?

BERT: Eh, about normal, thank you sir. And yourself?

P. R.: Mmm? *(Hands Bert empty glass)* Now what's your poison? Spirits? *(At mention of "spirits" Bert drops glass. He is shaking)* Or wine? *(Turns as glass drops)*

BERT: Yes, sir. Please. Excuse me, sir. Just the strain.

P. R.: This train? Nonsense just a trifle bumpy. Someone turning over in their sleep, probably. *(About to pour wine into glass)* A minor problem. *(Bert drops glass again)* Come along, man. Pull yourself together. Steel your nerves. *(Bert drops glass with one hand and catches it with the other)*

P. R.: *(Pours out wine)* I think you need this. Cheerio.

BERT: *(Unwilling to be alone)* Where are you going, sir?

P. R.: Eh? No, Cheerio, Down the Hatch, Mud in your Eye, Bottoms' up, or whatever you chaps say as you swill back your pints.

BERT: O, I'm no beer drinker, sir. O no. As a matter of fact, my palate has always gravitated towards wine, actually. I'm considered quite a "connosoire" back home. (*P. R. chokes, unnoticed, into his glass*) Yes, in fact I went to a three-day, wine-tasting coach trip round the vineyards of La France "la-nny den-ee-aire". (*Anglo-french pronounciation*) In my own humble way, I count myself quite an expert on the subject. (*He takes a sip, rolls it round ostentatiously on his tongue? Gargles violently and swallows it*) Mmmm.

P. R.: And how would that rate in your excellent judgement?

BERT: (*Sipping and sniffing*) I'd say a light, dry, mature vintage. Crisp, but slightly fruity, with a faintest of rare bouquets. Mmm, a superior, cheeky little number, undoubtedly from the St. Emilion region of France.

P. R.: Would you now?

BERT: Probably a '77, though-possibly, just possibly '79. Both good harvests.

P. R.: Actually it's a litre and a half of Sainsbury's cheap plonk I always keep for the staff... Ha ha ha. Ghastly stuff. (*Uncorks a rare mouton for himself*)

BERT: I fail to see what is so funny, sir. It was a slight error of judgement, perhaps...

P. R.: Bert, you couldn't tell a Chateau Rothschild '47 from a glass of Ribena. And even if you could, what earthly good would it do you?

BERT: One can learn the finer things of life. Learn taste and discrimination. Even... aspire to higher positions.

P. R.: So that's what you're after. Bert, some were born great. Others achieve it by a mixture of brains, bluff, and vicious, bloody-minded arrogance, and the rest, like yourself, might just as well forget it.

BERT: O come on, after all we done together... I was hoping...

P. R.: Were you now?

BERT: Well, it wouldn't be fair, otherwise.

P. R.: (*Knocking back the mouton*) Life, Bert, is not fair. We do not live in a perniciously suffocating egalitarian society of Commissariats. This is England. I did not learn to appreciate the finer things of life on a day-trip to a Dieppe Hypermarket. With me it is second nature, absorbed through the stitching of the old school tie, and the osmosis of taste that comes with breeding, Bert, and having forelocks continually tugged in front of one's eyes.

BERT: But we've always been like that. (*Holds up crossed fingers*) I don't get it.

P. R.: And the tragedy is, you never will. Try skimming through "Who's Who", you'll soon find out what's what. Hard luck, Bert. You'll never make it to the Lodge, and I shouldn't think your little Mafioso will welcome you back.

GHOST'S VOICE: Don't let turd get away with that.

BERT: You don't mean 'the Union', sir?

P. R.: (*Has a spasm*) Argh, don't say that word!

BERT: No, sir. Sorry, sir. Apologise, sir.

P. R.: *(Going with drinks trolley)* I'll leave you to the, eh, St. Emilion, shall I? Ha ha ha.

BERT: I'm not sorry. I'm not sorry. So there Union, union, union. You superior stuck-up sodding son of a b... Burgundy. I bet *you* don't know where to get the best jellied eels in London on a Saturday night after the pub's shut. Well, *I* do, and I'm not telling. I've got my roots too. *(Pause)* Trouble is, I don't own the ground they're in. Think you're so clever don't you? Think you got it all. *(Pause)* You have. But not for ever. Not for much longer. O no. I'll get my own back on you, you shitbag. Just you wait. *(Bert exits saying the last few lines)*

(P. R. enters and addresses the audience)

P. R.: I know you're not really taking this lot seriously. But, just in case some of you are misguided or plain stupid enough to think "Yes, there might be something in what they say", I think it's time I put you right. Very right. For instance, this analogy between quantum physics and a potential Utopia—I hope you're all taking it with a pinch of sodium chloride. It might be academically interesting to people who like to think of themselves as trendy, liberal intellectuals, but, as always, these parallels are carried too far. I mean, the whole thrust of quantum physics lies in the theory that we actually create the world around us—well really! Patterns of mind equal patterns of matter—honestly! That we don't just sit back and observe the world, we participate in the making of it—words fail me! The world *is*, whether we like it or not. You may not like some if it. Nor do I, believe me. But *I* can change it. That's what you elected me for. And may I compliment you on your choice. I know it's hard these days. You look at a candidate and think—"Would I buy a used car from him?" Fair enough. It's a good yard-stick for governing this country and playing a vital world-role in a time of crisis and imminent destruction. So, get nice and comfy, watch this riff-raff, and have a good laugh at their expense, but leave the rest to me. Thank you.

(He exits one side as Phyllis enters behind Polly)

PHYLLIS: So now there's a spontaneous uprising of the proletariat?

POLLY: Not so's you'd notice it. They looked up, grunted and went back to their crosswords.

PHYLLIS: O. Do you think if I delivered my lecture...

POLLY: No! I don't.

PHYLLIS: So what's our next move?

POLLY: *(Thinking fast)* People *will* mobilise round a single issue.

PHYLLIS: And in doing so will make other connections!

POLLY: Right. So we'll use the waste.

PHYLLIS: Alert them to it?

POLLY: Shove it under their noses.

PHYLLIS: But that's suicidal. Without precautions, the radiation could...

POLLY: That's why I brought this. *(Brings out a space-type suit and helmet)* And a book on it.

PHYLLIS: *(Picking up book and flicking through)* "Zen and the Art of Handling Nuclear Waste".

POLLY: But it's all scientific language.

PHYLLIS: Let's see. Mmmm. Mmmm. Mmmm.

POLLY: Good read, is it?

PHYLLIS: Fascinating.

POLLY: Tremendous. Well, tell me what it bloody-well says.

PHYLLIS: You wouldn't understand.

POLLY: I know that. Translate.

PHYLLIS: You know, Polly, it might be better if I handled this part, since I...

POLLY: Look, don't start taking over.

PHYLLIS: But you don't seem to realise the risk...

POLLY: It's important for me that I do it, right?

PHYLLIS: Very well. Number one... Mmm Mmmm Pi R^2 Mmm Mmm... millicurie disintegration... Mmm Mmm ionisation density... Put on the suit. *(Polly raises eyes to heaven and starts to put it on, helped by Phyllis. They talk as they do it)* I think it's this way round. Poor Mrs and Uri. They don't look very cheerful.

POLLY: Joys of being a family.

PHYLLIS: Is that another of the things you don't like? It is rather basic to our society, isn't it?

POLLY: 'S right. You trying to say that recommends it?

PHYLLIS: Well no, but still... do you have a family?

POLLY: Not that I wanna think about. *(Starts to mimic)* "Aha, I see, so you never played Happy Families, that's why you're knocking it". They always trot that one out. It seems to be the cause of everything, from revolutionary activity to piles.

PHYLLIS: Who says that?

POLLY: The head doctors. "Humm, tell me, when you were ten did you fall in love with other girls?"

PHYLLIS: How silly. It's quite normal at that age.

POLLY: It's normal at any age. *(There is a silence. Phyllis opens her mouth several times as if to speak, but then thinks better of it)*

PHYLLIS: I never saw much of my family, so I suppose I always had a yen for it.

POLLY: They split up?

PHYLLIS: O yes, years ago. I always spent term times at school and hols with Aunt Edith and her friend. She was a jolly decent old girl and we got on awfully well actually. But the other girls always used to talk about their folks, so I felt as though I was missing out.

POLLY: Don't sound like it.

PHYLLIS: You're home life was... difficult then?

POLLY: No. Blissful. Ecstatic even, so long as you kept the curtains shut and didn't scream too loud, so's next door didn't hear. Then I realised the same thing was happening next door.

PHYLLIS: But surely your bad experience...

POLLY: *(Exploding)* How can millions of families go through hell, and they still say "You're all having bad experiences". Why don't they realise that the Family as we know, and don't bloody love it, *might* just be the bad experience. But they're just concerned not to rock the boat.

PHYLLIS: Who's the they? The head doctors again?

POLLY: No, the bloody social workers.

PHYLLIS: Aren't they just trying to help out?

POLLY: You lot never cease to amaze me. You fuck the whole world up, and everything that's in it, then you kindly come along and offer us the benefit of your advice. Screw that.

PHYLLIS: *(Subdued)* Your gloves.

POLLY: Ta. You got the book?

PHYLLIS: Yes. Are there any instructions you wish me to carry out, just in case you don't...

POLLY: *(Starting to go out)* Yeah. Make sure Uri takes his medicine.

PHYLLIS: Polly *(Polly is stopped by her tone)* Don't patronise me. I am not personally responsible for all the ills that have befallen you. I admit it's time I did some soul-searching, but I am not going to be treated as your doormat, or let myself be manipulated by guilt. Now, is there anything I can usefully do while you're away?

POLLY: *(After a silence)* Yeah, one very important thing. Get the guard out of the way.

PHYLLIS: Bert. That'll be a pleasure.

(They exit)
(Enter P. R.. He addresses the audience)

P. R.: It hasn't escaped my notice that this train is tipping rather dangerously to the left. Anyone else found a general bias in that direction? (My Left is your Right, remember). But now, looking at you all I can see why, of course. It's the way you're all sitting and looking at this. If everyone could just slide along to the extreme right of their seats, and perching on the right-hand buttock, lean over with your heads tilted at a 90° angle. That's it. Now close your left eye. Capital. That should give you a proper perspective.

(He exits. Bert enters and paces in an agony of doubt)

BERT: To be or not to be a grovelling, arse-licking class traitor, that is the question. Whether it isn't bloody stupid to give up a smart uniform and a fat wage packet...

PHYLLIS: *(Entering)* Hey, nonny nonny no, hey... ah, Bert. When we stopped back there, some of the passengers gathered some wild flowers. Aren't they super? I thought we should forget our differences you and I, so I brought a small bunch for you.

BERT: *(Taut with nerves)* Get thee to a Laboratory.

PHYLLIS: Look here, I was only trying to be chummy. You know—"Make up, make up, never do it again", sort of thing. *(Bert suddenly bursts into tears and clings to an astonished Phyllis)* Bert, Bert, unhand me. Or I shall have to warn you I am a karate Black Belt. I do not permit male personages to come this close. In fact, if you don't take your paws off, I shall resort to a knee in the... you know where.

BERT: I haven't got any you know whats you know where. I'm really Bertha, not Bert. Under this uniform I'm just the same as you. Look I'll show you. *(Starts to undo jacket)*

PHYLLIS: Bert, button yourself immediately. *(Sniffs)* You've been drinking. That's it, isn't it? Aha, just as I thought. A litre and a half of Sainsbury's plonk.

BERT: *(Advancing menacingly)* Don't you bleeding start. I've had enough.

PHYLLIS: Right. I warned you. *(She does an impressive throw and lands Bert on the floor)* I shall report your behaviour to Poxy Percy... I mean to your boss.

BERT: *(Belligerently)* Don't you dare, or I'll throw the book of byelaws at you. You'll be doing concurrent sentences for the next thirty years.

PHYLLIS: For what?

BERT: For everything. From pulling communication cords to having a widdle while the train's in the station.

PHYLLIS: Outrageous.

BERT: It's your own fault. Going to report me, was you? After I'd gone and confided my biggest secret to you. *(She begins to break down again)* My secret of the sensational scandal of my true sexual identity.

PHYLLIS: Bert, you've been reading too many scummy Sunday newspapers.

BERT: It's true, I tell you. No one else knows in the world... in this world. I've kept up my disguise night and day for years. Even buying razors and shaving cream regularly. Getting Tampax by mail order. I had to, to get this job. But it's a secret, see. A secret.

PHYLLIS: *(Archly)* I have never narked in my life. Guides' honour. Not even when Bully Bellinger set fire to the chemmy lab. with a Bunsen burner. So there.

BERT: *(Muttering tearfully)* Never understand. *(Blows nose)* Different class.

PHYLLIS: Mmm? O yes. I was in Fourth Remove and Bully Bellinger was in 5 B. Now, come along, dry your eyes. Tell me what's wrong, woman to... eh woman.

BERT: There's them what's Eton and them what's not.

PHYLLIS: I've got a cheese roll in my bag if...

BERT: There's them as got Landed Seats and them what manage in a two up two down.

PHYLLIS: O I think everyone on the train's got a seat, Bert. They're all quite comfy.

BERT: There's them what gets to Balliol...

PHYLLIS: Bally old what?

BERT: And them what get dumped in a Tech. There's them with silver spoons and them with MacDonald's plastic forks rammed down their gobs.

PHYLLIS: (Gently) O, O, I see what your driving at.

BERT: (Bitterly) No you don't. They know how to talk, to explain themselves. Articulated, they are. Like you. (Phyllis looks uncomfortable) Me, I've always felt safer with the Byelaws in me hand. It's all written down there, see? And if anyone argues, you show it to them, triumphant-like, sort of superior-like. You're right and they're wrong. Know exactly where you are.

PHYLLIS: Yes, I see. Of course.

BERT: But the thing is... the thing is it's people like him what writes the byelaws, and if his royal, bleeding highness wants to he can change them, like that. (Snaps her fingers) You can be announcing, same as usual, (Raises voice) "the 4.22 to Clapham Junction will be leaving from Platform Three", when some bright spark'll up and say—"You're wrong, Bert, it's all changed". "Since when?" "Since five minutes ago. Didn't no one tell you? They've changed it. It's now the 4.28 to Balham South from Platform Eight". See what I mean?

PHYLLIS: (Soberly) Yes.

BERT: (The tears reappearing) But it's my own fault. As the ghost of my dear, dead mother, what just now appeared to haunt me, said—"Bert, thou are traitor t' union, and t' historic struggle." (Weeps)

PHYLLIS: There, there. It's alright. No, what am I saying? It's not all right. It's all wrong. You're right. (Pause while Bert blows her nose and Phyllis thinks) (Aside) Wait. Phyllis, this could be some trick to give yourself away. Of course. Why should Bert suddenly have a change of heart? And a change of sex? Ahem, Bert?

BERT: (Miserably) Yes.

PHYLLIS: How many times do you have to flush the loo before your cardboard applicator goes down?

BERT: Twice, at least. Or once, if I scrunch it up really tight.

PHYLLIS: (Aside) Only a woman could possibly know that. But she could still be a spy, woman or not.

BERT: Why am I telling you all this, anyway. You'll just tell him. You're one of them.

PHYLLIS: But I am not one of... (*Catching herself*) Well, so are you.

BERT: Maybe, just *maybe*, I'm not no more.

PHYLLIS: Maybe I'm not no more... I mean, any more, either. Maybe I'm not on their side at all.

BERT: How can I trust you?

PHYLLIS: How can we trust each other? That's the problem.

TOGETHER: (*Facing different directions*) She could be a double agent. Hmm. But the thing is, I don't have to tell her everything. Little here, little there, as a test. See what happens. If she grasses I can always say I had my suspicions about her and was just testing. (*They turn to face each other*) Sister.

PHYLLIS: (*Aside*) I definitely won't tell him... eh, her, what Polly's up to right now. (*Aloud*) Well, the aim is to stop the train once and for all. So the first thing is to let everyone know what's going on. Then there'll be a spontaneous uprising of an outraged proletariat.

BERT: Huh. You'll get an eyebrow lifted, little grunt, then they'll all go back to their crosswords. Show 'em the waste. They won't be too happy then.

PHYLLIS: (*Suspicious*) You mean the... eh waste of resources, the waste of human potential... the...

BERT: Waste of time. No, like I said, give 'em a butchers at the 'you know what'. Shove it in their faces. Then the shit'll hit the fan. They'll have to get off their arses and do something then.

PHYLLIS: Yes, yes. (*Uncertainly*) Perhaps you're right. But that will be a last resort, of course. (*But Bert is looking at the flowers still in Phyllis' hand*)

BERT: These are beautiful, aren't they? You know I've always loved flowers. (*Takes them*) It was very kind of you to think of me. No one's ever done that before. (*Embarrassed by such intimacies, Bert puts her nose in them. Suddenly she yawns loudly*) Ooh, all of a sudden I've come over ever so sleepy. I can't hardly keep my eyes open. I feel just like a... long... snooze. (*Sinks to ground and snores gently*)

PHYLLIS: O my goodness. I'd quite forgotten the flowers. (*Tries to hold Bert up and shake her awake. Bert opens her eyes, smiles and takes another deep whiff of the flowers*) No, no. Don't do that. Don't smell them.

BERT: Beautiful smell. Thanksalot.

PHYLLIS: Yes, of course, don't mention it. (*She wrenches flowers from Bert's hand*)

BERT: My beautiful flowers.

PHYLLIS: I'll... I'll put them in a vase for you.

(*But Bert is already asleep, smiling*)

PHYLLIS: Bert, Bert. Don't go to sleep now, there's work to be done. Ah, well, I suppose she seems to be with us in spirit. Spirit! What was that she said about the ghost of her dead mother come to haunt her? Anything's possible on this train. Phyllis, perhaps this is just the opportunity to find out whether she's a 'jolly good sport' or a 'rotten sneak'. Now how was it she said her mother spoke? *(Tries it out)* Bert. No. Bert. Better. Bert. That's more like it. Ooh, this is exciting. Rather like the time I played the ghost of Hamlet's father in the School play. *(She stands behind Bert)* Bert. Bert.

BERT: Eh? What? Mum O mum, is't you again? Mine own dear mummy.

PHYLLIS: Aye, Bert. Answer me just one question.

BERT: Anything, mum.

PHYLLIS: Art thou still traitor t' struggle?

BERT: O no mum. I've turned over a new leaf. I've joined up in solidarity with the scientific woman, the daft looking one with the funny voice.

PHYLLIS: *(Looking annoyed)* She's a good 'un, Bert. Trust her.

BERT: Yes, mum.

PHYLLIS: And she don't look daft neither. *(Cuffs her round the ear)*

BERT: *(Sitting up and rubbing her ear)* Uh? Uh? Where am I? Mum? Mum?

PHYLLIS: No, it's Phyllis. Your mother had to leave unexpectedly.

BERT: *(Trancelike)* She must away 'ere break of day.

PHYLLIS: Eh, something like that. Now, Bert, I *know* you really are a good sort.

BERT: *(Still half-asleep)* You do?

PHYLLIS: Yes, and just to prove to you that I am... *(She pulls her to her feet, closes her eyes, puts one hand on her heart and holds a sleepy and confused Bert's high in the air with the other)*

> "By bully off and jolly dee
> And lob it up the pitch
> The girls can always count on me
> I swear I'll never snitch
>
> By midnight feast and dorm hi-jinks
> And lemon pud for lunch
> By secret pash and Head Girl's winks
> Forever I'm one of the bunch."

There, now you *know* you can trust me.

BERT: I do?

PHYLLIS: And if either of us have a secret message, the password is— "Friend of Dorothy". Right, well I'll sally forth into the First Class compartments and tell people what's afoot. Stir up their sense of British injustice and get them on our side. And to allay any suspicion, you must carry on as if nothing has happened. Just the same old Bert, you understand. *(She starts to stride off)*

BERT: Oi, oi oi. 'Ere.

PHYLLIS: *(Turning uncertainly)* Eh, does that mean 'cheerybye'?

BERT: No, it means 'Oi', 'none of that', 'come 'ere'. *(Phyllis returns)* You said—carry on the same like nothing's happened, right?

PHYLLIS: Yes, that's right. Shall I run over it ag…

BERT: Well, something has happened actually. I may look the same. I might act the same. But I'm not going to lose my job and my superhannuation, just to swop one guvner for another. Right?

PHYLLIS: Of course, you're absolutely right. We're a team, but with no Captain. *(Wistfully)* Or Games Mistress, either. I just thought, subject to your agreement, of course, that I'd get going on the First Class passengers, because I know how to approach them, that's all. You know, best way to chivvy them along and get them to play fair, so to speak. Whereas you… may not know quite the right… eh… angle to work on… so to speak.

BERT: Alright, we've got our different tasks…

PHYLLIS: But they're all of equal importance.

BERT: And no one tells no one what to do.

PHYLLIS: Agreed. I say, this is all jolly collective, isn't it, mucking in together.

BERT: *(Defensively)* Well, I got as much right as you to say what I want.

PHYLLIS: Absolutely. O, complete democracy is essential. Any attempts at coercion would be utterly reprehensible. We reject all authoritarianism and embrace egalitarian philosophy and practice entirely. We must start as we mean to go on. Taking into account the dialetical interchanges that will naturally occur en route.

BERT: *(After pausing)* Naturally.

PHYLLIS: Perhaps, if we lose complete contact… one of us should… eh…

BERT: Pull the communication cord.

PHYLLIS: Jolly good idea.

P. R.: *(Entering)* Ah, Bert, there you are. Apparently someone's been touting round the Second Class carriages fermenting rebellion. O, by the by, talking of fermenting, how was the St. Emilion, eh? Ha ha ha. *(Bert looks dangerous and mutters under her breath)*

PHYLLIS: *(In a desperate undertone)* Remember you've got to act normal, Bert.

BERT: Eh, very enjoyable, thank you… sir.

PHYLLIS: Has anyone been caught, eh, fermenting?

P. R.: Caught? O loads. Well, not exactly redhanded. But we've taken in a couple of carriages or so, under suspicion of passing on seditious information.

PHYLLIS: On what grounds?

P. R.: Possession of potentially offensive weapons. They all had mouths. Don't worry. We'll get to the bottom of this. The train's crawling with plain clothes. In fact, you can't tell who's who any more. Turns out half the people we've arrested are our own chappies. Still, the interrogations should give them a bit of exercise. Right, well I think now's the time for the Press to interview our Family. Take their minds off the furore in the corridors. Where the deuce has the girl gone now?

PHYLLIS: Eh... she's...

BERT: *(Looks quickly at Phyllis and realises Polly most be part of the plot)* Gone to the Buffet car. For tea.

P. R.: Tea? Splendid idea. A truly family setting. Mrs being mum over the teapot, and the young scholar making scientific chit chat with his personal tutor. And the girl being a pain in the...

PHYLLIS: Perhaps she should stay in the Buffet.

P. R.: Capital idea.

PHYLLIS: O, but then there'll be no one to manipul... eh, manage the conversation if it should flag.

P. R.: Good Lord, then she's the last person we'd want. There's something not quite true to life about her. Hmmm.

PHYLLIS: O well, at least the rest of the family are the real thing.

P. R.: True. But still, a nuclear family of two doesn't look very homey, does it? Would we really want to call this the cornerstone of our society? The rock upon which nation and Empire were built?

BERT: Nice dog. I like dogs. Here doggie.

PHYLLIS: Eh, be careful. She bites. About to have pups quite soon, apparently.

P. R.: O that's all we need over tea. A bitch giving birth.

BERT: Ah, look at her looking at us. You got lovely blue eyes, haven't you? Yes, you have. Lovely blue eyes. They say it's all in the genes.

P. R.: Bert. You're a genius.

BERT: *(Modestly)* Well, I always thought, given the right education...

P. R.: *(To Phyllis)* You're a scientist. You can give it a caesarean then turn the puppies into children. Two normal little kiddiwinks. Boy and girl, one of each, that's all we need. You can chuck the rest away.

PHYLLIS: But I'm a physicist, not a biologist.

BERT: *(Sadly)* I never did science at school. *(More brightly)* I was more on the artistic side myself. I always had a good imagination. So I joined British Rail.

P. R.: But you could put the human genes of Uri and Polly into two puppies, couldn't you?

PHYLLIS: You mean, take their cell tissue...

BERT: Bless you.

PHYLLIS: ... and implant it in two animals? Never.

P. R.: We pay well. In fact, it's one of the few real growth industries left. Ha ha ha.

PHYLLIS: No. It's entirely unethical.

P. R.: O go on. What's a little jiggling of genes between friends? Eh? Just a small re-arrangement of DNA?

VOICE: *(Taped)* I say, what's going on here. What's the delay?

P. R.: Nothing. Just a little genetic engineering on the line. No problem. *(To Phyllis)* You have the power to create a normal, happy nuclear family. Now what's unethical about that, eh? Nothing more natural.

BERT: Sir?

P. R.: *(Impatiently)* What is it, Bert?

BERT: A thought did strike me.

P. R.: *(Spasm)* Strike! Don't mention that word.

BERT: Beg pardon, sir. But I just thought that if it was all natural-like, this here happy nuclear family, why do you have to jiggle the genes?

P. R.: Bert, you are stupid. Don't ever think of becoming a father... Bert. Bert, of course. *(Inspiration hits him)* A father, that's what we need.

BERT: Eh?

P. R.: *(Very chummy)* Bert, wouldn't you say that Mrs is your cup of Maxpax?

BERT: Pardon?

P. R.: Granted. Look at her, Bert. Fancy her, eh? Just think, a wife to potter round your lonely little lemon and lavender fitted kitchen. Dashing away with her soothing iron. Filling it with love and freshly laundered linen. *(With distaste)* And acrylic. And just think of those two dear little children calling you 'Daddy'. Your very own family, Bert. Ready-made, off the peg and a superb fit. Cheap at the price.

BERT: B-b-b-but she's already married.

P. R.: O we can easily 'manage' that.

BERT: You can't mean...?

P. R.: Just take him off the computer. He will never have existed.

BERT: How did she get these two, then?

P. R.: The perfect wife. Even in conception she was quite immaculate. Now I think you two should get aquainted, while I stage manage this little charade for the photographers. *(He exits)*

PHYLLIS: Go on, Bert. It won't be for long. And please try and keep mum.

BERT: It's alright for you keeping mum, but I'm the one who's got to marry mum.

PHYLLIS: O no, that's alright. She's just a dummy.

BERT: Now look here, just 'cos she's not in your class, don't mean she ain't intelligent. It's all a matter of education.

PHYLLIS: No, she really is a dummy. Look. *(Phyllis shows her the back of Mrs. Bert screams. Then turns Uri round)*

BERT: So's he.

PHYLLIS: So's Pluto. It's all part of the conspiracy, you see, posing as the family, so that Polly could get on the train unsuspected and stir up the proletariat to revolution.

BERT: Not short-haired and burly, is she?

PHYLLIS: Eh, yes, she is as a matter of fact. Now you'll have to try and manipulate the dummies. I know it looks extraordinarily difficult, but perhaps if you had a little go at the doings inside...

BERT: Ahem, excuse me. It just so happens that the ancient art of ventriloquism is a little hobby of mine, what I learnt from a library book and do annually every year at the Station Master's Christmas do. (*Bert does some throat-clearing limbering exercises, screws up face and wiggles fingers*) Would you mind if I took this seat, madam.

MRS: O no, not at all. Plenty of room.

PHYLLIS: I say, Bert, that's jolly impressive.

BERT: Might I be permitted to introduce myself? I'm Bert.

MRS: Mrs. Pleased to meet you, I'm sure. This is my son, Uri.

(*Enter P. R. singing with a tray of Maxpax*)

P. R.: "Getting to know you
    Getting to know all about you... ". Wonderful picture. I want you to look as though you've been married for years when the photographers come.

MRS: Perhaps we should be having a row then.

P. R.: No, no. Carry on. (*Singing*)

    "Happy talking talking
    Happy talk
    Talk about things you'd like to do..."

BERT: (*In undertone*) I know what I'd like to do to you.

(*They all settle down*)

P. R.: Just wait for the tea to brew. (*An awkward pause*)

PHYLLIS: Well, this *is* jolly.

MRS: Yes, I'm always ready for a good strong cuppa.

PHYLLIS: Well, perhaps we could open them up now.

P. R.: (*Highly irritated*) We're waiting for the photographers. Don't want the whole lot guzzled before they arrive. They're not cheap, you know. 30 pence a cup. (*He looks round for offers of recompense. No response*) Well, it's my treat. Should get some nice shots of a really English family occasion. Yes, an experience shared right across the nation. As the clock chimes four o'clock and everything stops for that chink of china and the pleasant tinkle of leisurely, informed conversation.

MRS: No, 3.30.

PHYLLIS: I beg your pardon.

MRS: Teabreak. 3.30 in our works. I always gulp mine down. You can feel it scalding all the way down your insides.

PHYLLIS: But that's ever so bad for one's health. Wouldn't you agree Mr P. R.?

P. R.: Mm? O yes. Good health is a duty for any woman with a family, you know.

MRS: Have to, dear. Only get ten minutes. If you want a fag and a wee wee and be back at your machine by the time the buzzer goes. *(P. R. coughs loudly)* I mean, you can't keep a full bladder for 2 hours, can you? Can't keep your legs crossed and hope for the best. *(Chuckles. Bert is obviously enjoying every moment of P. R.'s discomfort and distress)* 'Cos if you're half a minute late back, you get 15 minutes docked off your pay.

PHYLLIS: But that's positively Victorian.

MRS: Used to be half hour, only management gave in over that.

PHYLLIS: I should jolly-well think so.

MRS: Was either that or a pay rise. They weren't stupid, eh? Eh, Mr. P. R.?

P. R.: Quite. *(In undertone)* Bert, you'll have to control her tongue when the Press arrive. Can't you pull any strings?

BERT: I'll do the best I can, sir.

MRS: Do you like a nice cup of tea, Bert?

BERT: O yes. Nothing that brings so much pleasure. As I sip my tea I'm always reminded of wood and leather.

PHYLLIS: Ah, willow bat on leather ball. Cricket, you mean.

BERT: No, leather boot and wooden truncheon, pickets, I mean. Always get a good cuppa in the coach after a punch-up.

P. R.: *(In furious undertone)* Bert, are you trying to catch me out?

BERT: No, sir, just trying to make pleasant tinkling conversation.

P. R.: Ah, the photographers have arrived at last. Now look jolly everyone.

PHYLLIS: I'll be mum, shall I? Save you the trouble of getting up Mrs. *(She opens the maxpax and pours milk, etc.)* Do have an over-priced stale cheese sandwich. *(To Bert. However, Bert has Mrs in one hand and a maxpax in the other)*

BERT: I don't actually think I could manage one right now.

P. R.: Bert, psst, Bert, do tell your beloved the cup goes on the right and the tea plate on the left. Touch of class, I think is called for.

BERT: Maxpax on right, polystyrene lid on left, sah!

PHYLLIS: *(Still being mum)* Isn't Uri going to have tea with us? *(Bert looks at her in alarm and makes faces. Puzzled, she makes faces back)*

P. R. Yes, give him a shake, Bert. I think a photie or two of him and his devoted tutor making scintillating observations on Einstein would be quite a coup.

BERT: I should say it would.

PHYLLIS: Wakey wakey, Uri. *(Bert is now desperately making faces. Phyllis shakes her head in non-comprehension, mouthing a "what?")*

BERT: *(In undertone)* I've only got two bleeding hands. *(Holds up maxpax and jerks head towards Mrs)*

PHYLLIS: Oh. Ohh. Poor boy, he looks so sound asleep.

MRS: Ah, shame to wake him really, bless him.

PHYLLIS: I'm sure a photo of the lad asleep in the bosom of his family would be just as... *(She breaks off suddenly and screams, pointing)* Argh. There's someone outside the window. *(They all turn and stare)* They must be hanging off the roof of the train by their fingertips.

BERT: Got to be a byelaw against that.

P. R.: If there isn't I'll write one.

MRS: I think whoever it is is trying to get in, you know.

P. R.: Just someone bumming a free ride. A hanger-on.

PHYLLIS: Must be hanging on for dear life.

MRS: Hadn't we better open the window and let them in?

P. R.: I think not. Especially with our spotless upholstery in here. Their face is black. With soot.

PHYLLIS: But she or he could get very hurt. Don't you think we should do something?

P. R.: Quite right. *(He knocks on the window)* I say clear off, will you. There's a good chap.

BERT: She or he seems to be saying something.

MRS: Water, water.

PHYLLIS: Are you going to faint?

MRS: No, they're asking for water.

BERT: Poor devil.

P. R.: Only British Rail tea, I'm afraid. Give them some of that, shall we? Then perhaps she or he will leave us in peace. Yes, no matter what the situation, tea is a great comfort.

MRS: But it's cold.

P. R.: Have any of you got a bit left in the bottom? Perhaps the ladies could collect it all up and give it to the poor fellow. *(To audience)* Any of you out there got any slops you don't want? Bits with ash in you didn't fancy? Powdery after-taste you spat back? Come along. Be charitable. Dig deep for this poor unfortunate person on the outside.

PHYLLIS: Well, if you're not going to help her or him to come in, I am, at least, going to get them a *hot* cup of tea.

P. R.: No, no, bad move. You'll have them all crawling over the windows like flies, demanding this, that, and the other. Here, old chap, we've all rallied round and come to your aid.

BERT: There can't be half a cup there.

MRS: And it's stone cold.

BERT: She or he's saying something else.

PHYLLIS: What is it?

P. R.: Some mumbo jumbo meaning "thank you", no doubt.

MRS: Sounds more like "screw you".

P. R.: Best thing is not to look. They won't be there much longer anyway.

PHYLLIS: Why not?

BERT: Tunnel coming up.

PHYLLIS: What!!

P. R.: If I might be allowed to say a few words. Of course we are all concerned about this situation. But we have done our best, and that is all anyone can do. Any attempt at rescue would be hazardous and not in our own interest rate.

PHYLLIS: But it's a life at stake.

P. R.: Of course, you have every right to feel emotional about this, but I can't afford such a luxury. It's my job to see a balance is maintained and that's what I've done. The cost of their life against our cost of living—forget it, the price is too high.

PHYLLIS: I'm sorry but this is monstrous.

BERT: I thought we was keeping mum. (In undertone)

PHYLLIS: I feel I really have to speak out.

P. R.: A thinking woman, but, alas misguided. Very. Allow me to point you in the right direction on this subject. (Singing)

> There'll always be a Them and an Us
> Them with nothing and Us with surplus.
> Our standard of living would be halved
> If they didn't do the noble thing and starve.
> The tea in your pots would cost a packet
> If we didn't work the same old racket.
> Now don't plead innocence of exploitation
> Howdya think we keep down our own inflation?
> To First and Second Class it must have occurred
> There's yet another one—and that's the Third.
>
> There's Us and there's Them
> Don't let them kid you—we're not the same.
> And if you're buying, say, coffee or rice
> Don't muck things up and pay the proper price.
> There was a time they'd accept a bead
> Now they want cash—could you credit such greed?
> So we reckoned it was cheaper if we were gonna trade
> To bleed 'em dry, then give them aid.
> But while our market's strong and we've got our share
> Let's be honest—do you really care?"

(Song—The Colonial Earl Grey)
(The lights go down after the song and P. R. is found in the same position)

P. R.: But while our market's strong and we've got our share. Let's be honest—do we really care?

PHYLLIS: Yes, I care. When you do your monetary sums, do you ever count the cost to human life, health, happiness, integrity…

P. R.: Ah, now you're talking about those damned social sciences. All that doesn't come within the scope of economics.

PHYLLIS: Then it's time you redefined your economics. If it doesn't cover the *quality* of life then, I'm afraid, it is seriously lacking.

P. R.: If we started adding on the cost of all that lot, the entire World trade and banking system would collapse. It would be the death of the Free World—and any chance of making a quick bob. Look, let's face reality…

PHYLLIS: Alright. But whose reality are we going to face?

BERT: Look, out the window, they've got a gun.

P. R.: Nonsense. I would have been informed through the usual diplomatic channels…

PHYLLIS: Yes, you're right. It is a gun.

BERT: Everybody down. Duck. (*As Bert and Phyllis hit the deck, P. R. takes off Bert's hat, removes the gun and replaces the hat. Unnoticed by them he aims it at Bert's head. The lights go out. There is a bang and screams. The lights come on and Bert is lying on the floor. Phyllis is staring at the window. P. R. puts the gun in his pocket*)

PHYLLIS: She or he has gone.

P. R.: Going through the tunnel must have knocked her or him off. (*Phyllis shivers*) A fitting end. Back to the blackness from whence it came.

PHYLLIS: O goodness, Bert's been hit. (*Rushes to her*) But where?

P. R.: For reasons of Public Safety we can allow no more shameful demonstrations of this kind. And above all, we shall have to severely restrict people like that on or near this train. I'm very concerned about the danger to you all from such brutes. And especially to our poor, hard-pressed public servant here. God rest his soul.

BERT: 'Ere not so fast. I ain't dead yet. The bullet went through me hat.

PHYLLIS: Thank goodness.

P. R.: Quite. What's happened to Mrs and Uri? They haven't moved a muscle. They're just sitting there like two dummies.

PHYLLIS: O dear, the bullet must have gone through the hat, then ricocheted through Uri into Mrs. Poor devils.

P. R.: This won't get you an extra Widower's Allowance, you know.

PHYLLIS: (*Examining the hat*) Strange. This hole in Bert's hat. If one hadn't been quite sure, one would think the shot came from… this direction. (*She stands where P. R. stands*)

P. R.: Impossible. He must have been dancing round in a circle at the moment of impact.

PHYLLIS: And it's singed, as though the shot were fired from very close by.

BERT: Let me see. The hole's in the back and I was looking at the window. There was only one person behind me…

P. R.: Let's not jump to conclusions.

PHYLLIS: Is that a gun in your pocket?

P. R.: I'm certainly not pleased to see you.

BERT: And that was you. You tried to kill me.

P. R.: Have your Widower's Allowance.

BERT: After all my loyalty over the years. *(Bert advances on him)*

P. R.: Now look here, I will not be intimidated.

BERT: Take that. *(Bert hits him on the head with his hat)* And that, for all the lies you told me. And that *(Hits himself)* for believing them. *(Bert is driving P. R. back and out)* And that, for doing all your dirty work. And that, for getting nothing but humiliation in return. *(As they exeunt)*

PHYLLIS: Into battle, Bert. We've got them on the run. *(Holding gun)* Now I too shall be a heroine. My time has come. I shall hijack the train. Holding the gun a mere three inches from the driver's head I shall order him to stop the train immediately, or else. I shall be fair. I shall fire three warning shots into the air. And then the fourth... into his sandwiches. But then the... the fifth... O dear. Pull yourself together, Phyllis. This is a revolution. I'll just have a little practice first. This is your first warning... *(Shuts her eyes)* On your marks, get set, go. *(Loud bang)* O this brings back memories. Feet on the line, gels. Ready? Steady...

POLLY: *(Entering in waste gear she immediately dives to the floor)* Don't shoot.

PHYLLIS: *(With a scream)* Polly. Thank God you're back. I was practising to hijack the train and...

POLLY: It's O.K. It worked. *(Both very excited)* The passengers rose as one woman.

PHYLLIS: Stirred to action by the thought that they had, unknown to them, lost all civil liberties...

POLLY: No, they were scared shitless by the lump of waste. Then you'll never believe this—that guard, Bert...

PHYLLIS: Bertha.

POLLY: ... suddenly comes marching up. I was all ready to do him...

PHYLLIS: Her.

POLLY: ... over. When he...

PHYLLIS: She.

POLLY: ... gathers up all the passengers and leads them off to the front of the train to stop the driver. She?

PHYLLIS: Yes, he's really a she. I'll explain later. O good old Bertha, alone and triumphant at the head of an historic struggle.

POLLY: No, she was arm in arm with this transparent woman in white.

PHYLLIS: Mum. *(This causes Polly to look round and see the dummies slumped)* I do love a happy ending.

POLLY: This is just the beginning. Hey, what's happened to Mrs and Uri?

PHYLLIS: Dead. The bullet ricocheted... *(Polly stares)* Well, that's what I told Poxy Percy, anyway. *(Polly is putting them away)*

POLLY: Where *is* Slime Face? You didn't let him slither away, did you? (*A suspicious-looking figure in B. R. uniform is seen making for the front of the stage and trying to mingle with the audience*)

P. R.: Tickets please. Have your tickets ready, please. This is the Double Cross to King's Gloucester Express… (*Polly has walked up to him and removed his hat*) All change. (*He talks fast and smoothly*) I see your point. The 125 is a rigid, inflexible, outmoded, phallic fallacy, unable to join together its own compartments, or connect with anything outside of itself. But I'm different. I can bend over backwards to suit you (*Does it*), turn conceptual somersaults (*He does that*), perform moral cartwheels (*Does it*), political turn-arounds (*Swirls and lands beside them*), and in fact, switch sides before you've even noticed. That's why you need me. Communication is your problem. I can help you there. You want your ideas heard and intelligently discussed, right? First they have to be packaged. That's simple enough. Now it's got to be glossy. That's where you lot always go wrong. You need a lot of hype and promo. "Hey baby, get a load of this. It's the sell-out, eh, sale of the century". (*During the next speech they advance on him, forcing him up the ramp to the top*) Just off the top of my head. How about a real blitz of commercials on the telly. A woman striding along a beach that's swarming with wild-life. Long, blonde hair streaming behind her… ah, no, racist? Right, she's Asian. Long, black hair flowing in the breeze like the Sunsilk Ads. In one corner of the screen, a windmill energy generator. A surge of synthesiser chords, to prove this is a society that incorporates the new technology; just in case some people were worried you wanted to take them back to the Stone Age. (*He builds the story*) And then, a thunder of hooves and a man gallops up behind her on a piebald horse and swoops her into the saddle… eh, no, sexist. Perhaps, it's a man walking, long black hair in the wind, and a woman comes galloping up and gently, but firmly lifts him into… eh, no, heterosexist. Perhaps it's two men… or two women… or perhaps the person should be galloping, with the horses on top. Mmm, have to think about that one. (*They advance, he hurries on*) No. What about the other tack? All the things you don't like, the nasty, smelly, underarms of society. Think of the impact it would have, if we could get it into the top ten pop video charts. Let's see. Got it! Packed crowd of hungry unemployed; blurs into shot of battery factory with a hen trying to move her wing. Cut to the worst bit of a porno nasty. Don't want to turn the stomach, so give it lots of soft focus. Then a series of shots—X-ray of cancerous lung, either from nuclear exposure, toxic waste or simply standing in a traffic jam at rush-hour, leave them to draw their own conclusions. Camera angle widens to reveal the X-ray is hanging in hospital ward, now deserted. Slowly pans ward. Cobwebs everywhere, paint peeling, flies buzzing round a solitary bedpan, dust sheets and silence. Except for the rhythmic squeaking of a rocking wheelchair. Camera zooms in on a single old woman, sitting alone, forgotten. Shades of Miss, sorry, Ms Haversham. Perhaps a copy of 'Great Expectations' in her lap.

Provide a moment of irony. The woman's mouth opens in silent plea and out launches a Pershing Missile in slow motion. *(He teeters on the edge as they stand threateningly before him)* How am I doing? Am I going down well.

POLLY: Hope so.

(Suddenly the toilet seat above his head begins to descend, he jumps down and somersaults into the bowl. The seat closes over him and there is the sound of flushing. Polly and Phyllis sit on the seat smiling)

PHYLLIS: You know, Polly, I've had the most exciting time of my life. It even beats Einstein. I do hope we can go on being friends, because I've never met anyone like you before. We are friends, aren't we?

POLLY: Comrades in struggle.

PHYLLIS: Oh. Does that include being best chums, too?

POLLY: What you trying to say?

PHYLLIS: O, nothing much... I've so enjoyed doing subversive things. One could get quite a taste for it. And our long chats have been a veritable mine of info. I wouldn't have missed them for the world.

POLLY: You can get all that out of books easy enough.

PHYLLIS: Yes, o yes, of course, I shall. Rather. But... we could still meet sometimes and have a chinwag, couldn't we? I mean, you can't sort of... feel the same way about a book.

POLLY: Shall we see how it goes? *(Suddenly from below the toilet seat P. R.'s voice emerges)*

P. R.: *(Muffled voice)* I got it. This is going to be a winner. It'll slay them in the aisles. Giant motion picture. Enough stars to sink a battlesh... Greenpeace ship. Big name director, the works. A heartwarming, innocent love story set in a small Welsh valley—"How Green Can You Be?" Last take—a lift full of multi-racial miners, men and women, emerging into the daylight. Close-up of pit pony blinking in the sun. Always gets them. Sleepily the miners wipe the sweat from their brows. Suddenly their eyes light up. Ahead, atop a green hill, stands a huge solar panel, looking discreetly like a tree. A cheer goes up as they hug each other, throwing down their Davey lamps and their lunch boxes, with the half-eaten Sesame spread and seaweed sandwiches in. The cry goes up—"Enough jobs for us all in the valleys with solar energy and up yours to the Coal Board"...

POLLY: What do you reckon?

PHYLLIS: Rather like one's cardboard applicator, always goes down second time around.

(Sound of second flush and lights go out. Cast take a bow then, instead of going off, do last song—Now Wash Your Hands, Please)

THE END

ROCK SONG LYRICS

OWLS ONLY

The rails
Steel quiet as they steal quiet load the side cars
Behind the hush shut shed door on this particular night train.

Cast vast in the forecourt glow,
Filmy oil pools simmer
The days fag end
In the sump-black slump-backed night.
The station clock points the finger
A whistle cuts the night
And the great bulk lurches into monstrous motion.

The drum, the drums
The cargo comes
Into the deathlous, breathlous night
Moves soft and sure
Through field and moor
Fate of a freight
Owls only see

Towns slumber unaware of a distant
Dream-like rail wail
On and on and on over track and sleeper
Rural backwaters shed
Past the churchyard dead
And the nursery school
Too early for the bell.
Child bliss dream on, dream well
Cradled by the rhythm
Of wheel on steel
Cuckooned in a choo choo land.

WHITE OUT

Can the fabric
Take the strain
Can washed-out weave
Withstand the fray
Tearing fibres

Thread from thread
Can worn-out woman
Cope another day?

Rinsed and wrung
A task unsung
Pegged-out and hung
On a length of cord
That keeps her strung
That she aches to break
But its biological
Carries no reward

Behind the door of the big machine
The family dirt seeps into
A trickle of stain and locked in pain
Oozing quietly through and through

No mess, no fuss, its automatic
The fabric rots
Comfort-softened, made aromatic
Cleansed throughout
Yet somehow, it just don't wash

Start it up
The endless cycle begins
Start it up
The price goes up all the time
The Family wash is loaded
From the very start of our lives

Overloaded
The Family takes the strain
Overloaded
The stains they are ingrained
The White wash has begun
From the very start of our lives

THE COLONIAL EARL GREY

The Colonial Earl Grey amusedly sips
From a porcelain piece with an apricot glaze.
Talking of China, "More tea"?,

There's a pot at the end of the rainbow.
Coolly wiping his cucumber hands, he dips in for more,
A new taste, a Gentleman's relish, a capital dish!

The grand old Earl Grey
Who has ten thousand gilts
With a napkin carefully wipes his lips
And wipes them once again.
He takes the rich tea biscuit,
Nibbles with delight.
The burden carried by the man who's white
Ensures a healthy appetite.

Ah, the Duchess is home for tea!
The Chaw Chi Chee is on.
Tiffin and all that terrifin
Ritual sipping, China lipping,
"Sugar?" "Spiffing!", silver teaspoon tipping
And butter dripping off that scone,
That only we correctly pronounce.
A white silk glove hands me one.
The porcelain service is poised, old boy,
But oh, how the girl is slow!
"See, the bamboo enamel on that crockery".
"How charming!"
Picked up for a song in Nanking,
Reminds one of a different scene.

Nostalgia settles on the village green,
On our pleasant, leafy village green,
Where a cricketer stoops to field a ball
And a weary, bent back and a torn shawl,
(Of one who gathers a different leaf),
Recalls to the Earl Grey—he must check his shares
Of the multinational subsidiary.
Plenty, of course, but all that stands
Of an England he'd hoped would always be,
Where the clock stopped with petrified hands,
Where the clock stopped at a fossilised hour.
Time froze with a tea cup lifted
And a pinky stood at ten to three.

For some there's honey still for tea.

NOW WASH YOUR HANDS, PLEASE

It's just a theatre show
In a minute you'll go
Have a glass of wine
Criticise, despise, say it's witty and wise
It's been a waste of time

But can you afford to applaud
Seek the exit door
Go your separate way?
You feel disgust, say you must do something soon
Then adjust, as the memory fades.

CHORUS
Will you feel better, will you feel worse
Will you feel guilty, open your purse
Go home and cry, let it go by,
Say—don't look at me, nothing to do with me—
Don't wash your hands, please.

We say of course we care
We don't want to despair
So we'd rather not know.
We feel danger is near, but it's change we fear
More than the status quo.

If we turn away
Lies we consume today
Demand the payment due.
Our credit's running out, there is no doubt
The reckoning's coming soon.

Can we avert our eyes
Hope that we'll get by
Is it enough to survive?
When we know there's more to existence, resistance begins
To mean being alive.

Now Wash Your Hands, Please. Left to right: Jude Winter (P. R.), Hilary Ramsden (Phyllis), Tasha Fairbanks (Polly). Photo: Anita Corbin.

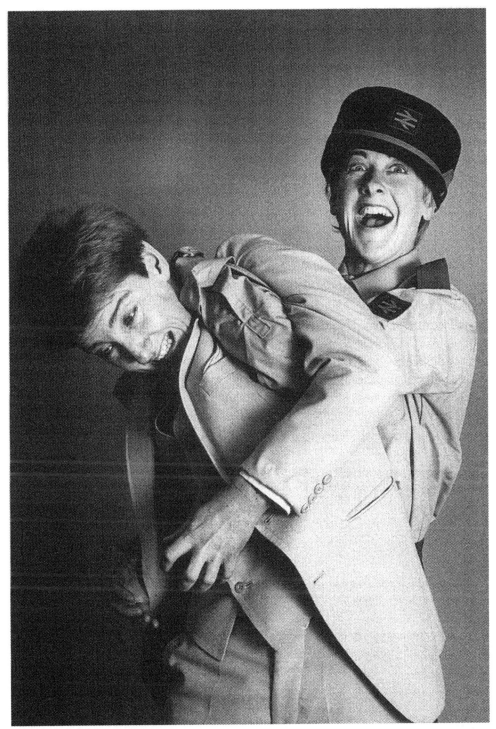

Now Wash Your Hands, Please. Left to right: Jude Winter (P. R.), and Tasha Fairbanks (Bert). Photo: Anita Corbin.

Now Wash Your Hands, Please. Tasha Fairbanks (Polly). Photo: Anita Corbin.

Other titles in the Contemporary Theatre Studies series:

This book is part of a series. The publisher will accept continuation orders which may be cancelled at any time and which provide for automatic billing and shipping of each title in the series upon publication. Please write for details.

www.ingramcontent.com/pod-product-compliance
Ingram Content Group UK Ltd.
Pitfield, Milton Keynes, MK11 3LW, UK
UKHW010021280225
455677UK00023B/736